SETTING THE ATMOSPHERE FOR THE DAY OF WORSHIP
II

Endorsements

"If you're looking for practical and wise counsel in leading your local church, then read this book. This is not a book that relegates worship to singing prior to the message. Instead, Dr. Girdler sets the context for the entire matrix of pastoral leadership needed in order for there to be the right atmosphere in the church for worship—in all its full-orbed meaning—to flourish."

Dr. George O. Wood
Chairman, World AG Fellowship, Springfield, MO

"Dr. Joseph Girdler has written an outstanding, hands-on, practical guide to developing the spiritual DNA of worship in the local church. His many years of national and international leadership among pastors and churches shine through on these pages. Pastor Joe specifies, step-by-step, the key areas and questions that church strategy must address, including the Spirit's guidance during worship. He understands that specific answers and strategies may vary from church to church, city to city, and region to region. However, every pastor and leadership team must wrestle with the questions Dr. Girdler raises in order to maximize the transformative impact of the worship service in the lives of people. This is a top-drawer read for every pastor and church leader."

Dr. Doug Oss
Director of Cordas C. Burnett Center for Biblical Preaching and Professor Emeritus of Biblical Theology

and New Testament, The Assemblies of God Theological Seminary/Evangel University, Springfield, MO

"When it comes to ministry life, sometimes what you really need is a *hand-on-the-shoulder, where-the-rubber-meets-the-road* kind of guidance from someone who's been there and lived to tell about it. *In Setting the Atmosphere for the Day of Worship – II,* Dr. Joseph Girdler offers exactly that, plus plenty of relatable stories and big doses of encouragement, to boot. This is a book that ministry leaders, especially those in pastoral roles, will find both applicable and invaluable.

Dr. Jodi Detrick
Author of The Jesus-Hearted Woman: 10 Leadership Qualities for Enduring & Endearing Influence, Seattle, WA

"This is a great practical help for pastors and church leaders to assess the 'first impression' people have when they come into church. If the saying, 'you never have a second chance to make a first impression' is true, it would serve every church well to look at how they 'do church' to allow people to encounter the Lord of the church rather than the flaws of preparation. This book provides very timely help."

Dr. Duane Durst
Superintendent, New York Assemblies of God, NE Region Executive Presbyter, AGUSA, Liverpool, NY

"*Setting the Atmosphere for the Day of Worship - II* is another insightful and practical guide offered by a fertile thinker and seasoned ministry leader. As I enjoyed every chapter, I kept saying, 'Yes, this is just the advice needed for leaders!' From polished shoes to prayerfulness in all situations, from holding the microphone during spontaneous moments in gatherings, to holiness without legalism, Pastor Joe invites us to love, to kindness, and to thoughtfulness in leadership. I recommend both volumes for leaders, placed within easy reach, right next to the Bible. In a culture obsessed with leadership, the author demonstrates that leaders are called ... and developed by the simple disciplines they practice. Along with the good advice, I pray that the ethos of these works will permeate the hearts of all who read them."

Dr. Charlie Self
Author and Minister,
Director of Learning Communities, Made to Flourish
Professor of Church History,
The Assemblies of God Theological Seminary/Evangel
University, Springfield, MO

"From a wealth of knowledge, education, and experience, Dr. Girdler approaches the practicality of ministry with implication and application. The principles taught are foundational to the smooth and professional running of Christ's Church. Wherever you are in life and ministry, there is more to learn and apply. *Setting the Atmosphere for the Day of Worship - II* and its prequel are a great place to start."

Darren M. Lewis
Lead Pastor, Calvary Christian Center AG, Louisville, KY

"Joseph Girdler offers a practical, yet thorough, set of perspectives about numerous aspects of the life of the church. He helps readers discover meaning in the often-overlooked details, while also learning to create a sense of vibrancy and expectation. The practical nature in which he writes makes application of the principles shared easy to implement. *Setting the Atmosphere for the Day of Worship - II* is a beneficial resource for every ministry leader, regardless of his or her tradition. I will be sharing this book with every pastor and leader in the Kentucky District Church of the Nazarene."

Dr. Brian L. Powell
District Superintendent, Kentucky District Church of the Nazarene, Louisville, KY

"I have known Dr. Joseph Girdler over thirty-five years and have found him to be a focused man of God. The first time I met Pastor Joe, I made a statement that I still say today: 'GREAT IS THE YIELD OF A FERTILE FIELD.' I've known Joe from the time he was a student, youth pastor, pastor, and now as Kentucky Superintendent of the Assemblies of God; all these years I have often enjoyed gleaning from Pastor Joe's God-given wisdom. His books and writings are well worth the investment to read and study. You will find his words practical and applicable to real daily ministry. Might I add, I found his wedding to Dr. Renee Vannucci Girdler to be the most powerfully spiritual wedding I ever attended. Joe's written words are like honey in the honeycomb."

Rev. Wade Martin Hughes, Sr.
AG pastor and featured writer on SermonCentral.com, with over 3,000 weekly sermon reviews and nearly 3.3 million total reviews of 1300 posted sermons from almost 100 nations. Smiths Grove, KY

"The message Pastor Joe offers in this book is priceless for ministers and leaders desiring to make a Kingdom impact in their local church and beyond. The principles offered in this book provide an opportunity for every pastor in every church to raise the bar in his or her ministry and experience the effectiveness God desires for each one. *Setting the Atmosphere for the Day of Worship - II* is written by a leader who understands the transformative power of God to change a person's life, offering people hope and direction.

Consequently, this book is not a sterile 'how-to' for church ministry, but a passionate plea for how a pastor can love the Church Jesus purchased with His blood."

Jeff Ferguson
Lead Pastor, First Assembly of God, Henderson, KY

"It was 1992 when I first met Dr. Girdler. Long hair, jeans, and flip-flops stood out as this Assemblies of God youth pastor joined a team of national youth leaders on a ministry trip to El Salvador. Evangelist Pat Schatzline, also a youth pastor at the time, preached, and Pastor Joe would sing in Spanish. It was quite remarkable, as he didn't speak fluently—nor does he still—a word of Spanish, but he had memorized in Spanish the words to the song with what he attempted in his 'unique' Hispanic dialect. What memories we made! *Setting the Atmosphere for the Day of Worship - II* is another memory maker, as Dr. Girdler has again offered a passionate, practical, and pastoral tool for equipping with concrete skills today's global Church leaders. Get both books in the series, *Setting the Atmosphere for the Day of Worship* and *Setting the Atmosphere for the Day of Worship - II* for your church leaders, and move your church to the next level.

Jim Wellborn
Assemblies of God World Missions, Builders International, Ozark, MO

"Dr. Joe Girdler mentions at one point in this book that when he came to Christ, he 'didn't have a lot to give,' but what he *did* have was *love*. Above all, that characteristic stands out in this man of God, this devoted husband, father, and grandfather, this passionate follower of Christ, this diligent learner—our gracious and joyful brother and pastor. He writes this book because he loves God, he loves the Church, and he loves people—regardless of where they are on their journey of faith. In that, this book is a great gift to all who read it, because it is born not out of desire for recognition but out of humble service to the One who has called and empowered him throughout faithful, decades-long service. Read on, friends, and enjoy this gift of love.

Dr. Lois Olena
D.Min. Project Coordinator and Associate Professor of Practical Theology and Jewish Studies, The Assemblies of God Theological Seminary/Evangel University, Springfield, MO

"As I read through pastor, church leader, and Dr. Joseph Girdler's newest book, *Setting the Atmosphere for the Day of Worship* – II, I thought of an *aha* moment a faculty member had a number of years ago after participating in a faculty development retreat on the deep integration of faith and learning; he said, 'I now get it. I can't give what I haven't received.' It was his personal realization that he could only nurture the spiritual lives of students if he was cultivating his own life of vibrant, lived-out faith. What Joseph Girdler offers us is what he has received over years of pastoral and leadership care for churches and larger faith communities. His insights come from a deep well of lived worship and from nurturing communities in a life of worship—and *we* are the beneficiaries.

Dr. Carol Taylor
President, Evangel University, Springfield, MO

"Dr. Joseph Girdler in his new book, *Setting the Atmosphere for the Day of Worship - II,* writes as one who truly strives for excellence in loving the Lord and leading His church. This work is the product of a seasoned leader in touch with the contemporary shifts that impact what a healthy church should look like. He has articulated twenty-three areas that impact not only the worship of the local church but the broader influence of the pastor and church to the surrounding community. The impact of the emphasis on worship provides a unifying purpose for the book. From conducting the actual worship experience to the personal attitudes of the pastor, from leading Board meetings to using social media, all these actions ultimately affect the atmosphere, the context, in which God's presence is encountered. Dr. Girdler has beautifully balanced his love for God and the Church with his love for people with respect to a healthy church model. He is helping influence this generation of pastors and church leaders by his solid and practical attention to essential principles of creating the atmosphere where God can be worshipped and experienced! This is a strategic resource both for beginning and experienced pastoral leaders!"

Dr. Gaylan Claunch
Superintendent, North Texas District, Assemblies of God

I have come to know "Dr. Joe" within the last few years and have been so enriched by his writings. He has the pen of a ready writer and an enjoyable way with words! There is flow and content both in practicality and Spirit enrichment in his penmanship. His twenty-six succinct chapters in *Setting* (first edition) and twenty-three concise chapters in *Setting II* is every pastor's pragmatic guide to doing church right in the twenty-first century. Whether urban, mid-town, or rural, there are a wealth of useful tools to "get it right" in today's Western culture. We have a radical commitment to excellence not because we are in competition with the pastor or church down the street but because our God is a God of excellence. They said of Jesus, "He does all things well." *Setting* and *Setting II* help us do all things well. Chapter 7 on *Personal Social Media: Dos and Don'ts* is worth the price of the book. I could go on and on about chapters on *Name*

Change, Leading From the Pastor's Home, Arminianism vs. Calvinism ... This is such a great resource for everyone, and especially our under-40 pastors! We are using this in Illinois!

Gary Grogan

Legacy Pastor, Stone Creek Church, Urbana, IL
U40 Network Director Illinois District AG Network
Bishop, SCC Francophone Network Churches
Board of Regents, North Central University

SETTING THE ATMOSPHERE FOR THE DAY OF WORSHIP
II

Joseph S. Girdler

Meadow Stream PUBLISHING

SETTING THE ATMOSPHERE FOR THE DAY OF WORSHIP II

Published in Crestwood, Kentucky by **Meadow Stream Publishing.**

ISBN   978-1-7337952-8-9   Paperback
ISBN   978-1-7337952-9-6   eBook

Meadow Stream
PUBLISHING

Dedication

This book is dedicated to my first grandchild, my grandson, James Hayes Girdler. Though I was in Egypt when he was born in New York City, I'll never forget the sense of thankfulness and prayers offered as I stood on a balcony that morning overlooking the grand city of Cairo. The time difference placed his birth in the early hours of the morning in Cairo and just a little past midnight in New York. I had faithfully and regularly prayed for James the nine months he was carried in his mother's womb. A few anxious moments took my heart immediately to the Lord in prayer again. Receiving the call that told of his healthy birth and his mom's health, I had an overwhelming awareness of God's love and a peace and tranquility few words can describe. My love for Baby James is beyond comprehension.

It was a few weeks later when I held him for the first time in my arms. For the "grands" out there reading this, you know what I felt; there is nothing like it. He has my blessing—a grandfather's blessing, you might say—and I pray God's closeness to him all the days of his life. What joy he brings!

I love you, James. The treasure of heaven is worthy. The Lamb of God is love and will surround you as He reveals himself to us daily. He will be your guide. He will make a way. He, my son, is faithful and true. Oh, what a life you have ahead. I can't wait to be there with you for some of this beautiful journey.

~All my love, always. Papa G.

Table of Contents

Acknowledgments

In 1982, my life found meaning, purpose, hope, joy, and contentment as I committed wholeheartedly to serve the Lord and pursue His Word and promises. At the time, I began attending a church, driving alone week to week, sitting unaccompanied most of the time the first number of weeks, giving little effort to intentionally getting to know those around me, just reckoning this thing called life. Soon, I found a community and was meeting and doing life with what would become forever friends and family, though many are now distanced by the years and rarely seen as our journeys have taken varying routes. Still, when we do re-connect, it's as if we were picking up thirty-five years ago like it was yesterday. That community, now scattered all over the globe, gave me optimism, confidence, and even anticipation for a promising life ahead that I could have never envisioned previously. They grew with me, laughed with me, dined with me, worked, played, prayed, cried, and whined (at times) with me—through the ebb and flow of learning to faithfully follow Christ. Many have never experienced this amazing gift from God: the Church. Believers may not always agree on every topic, especially through all the twists and turns of today's politics, or as they navigate the various genres of worship and church styles, but through this marvelous community, God's people find their understanding of Christ and His Church.

To all who poured into my life over those years, I consider each a friend and a meaningful collaborator in what have become my sentiments regarding the Church. Thank you for your touch on my life.

To my immediate family, Renee, Steven and Julia, and Rachel, I give always my love and devotion, as you forever will be my reason for living and my truest gifts from God. To the church staff at an early- to mid-1980s Lexington, Kentucky church who were the real deal and showed me Jesus so I could meet Him and know Him intimately— thank you. To the church members at a church our family gave sixteen of the best years of our lives to before I left to serve as a denominational superintendent—thank you. You know who you are. To the most amazing team members I have been privileged to work with after my move to the Louisville area for denominational leadership—thank you. To the mentors in my life at various stages of the decades— thank you. Names come to mind like my father, Hulen F. Girdler; my step-mom, Jessie Chandler Girdler; my brothers, Harry and David; and my late sister, Sue; my sisters-in-law, Sandy, and ... yes, another Sandy; my Jr. High and High School band director, Jack Walker; and a professor in my doctoral journey, Dr. Carolyn Tennant. Though they may not have known it, each molded me little by little. Today, this book, the second in the series, Setting the Atmosphere for the Day of Worship - II, is part of that seminal and pivotal shaping.

For technical and publishing support, Uberwriter's professionals, Brad, Hilton and Grant Rahme—from their desks in Louisville, KY, USA, to Cape Town, South Africa— helped shape my manuscript to the final product of this work. For chef-d'oeuvre editing—thank you, to Dr. Lois Olena.

May every reader find something within these pages to support and improve your labors for the Lord. While certain of the book's topics could appear random and indiscriminate in their inclusion to this work, I consider each one pertinent, sensibly essential, and culturally and contextually pragmatic for most worship and community environs. There is nothing more stunning than a vibrant local church and leaders who exemplify Christ. And, to the Christ follower, few things feel more lackluster than a church that does not exemplify such health. For the church-faithful ministries in urban, suburban, or rural areas—this book is for you.

Upon His imminent return, I trust the Lord will find us faithful and steady at our posts. When you fall, get back up. When you feel your calling is over, it is not. When you struggle to find yourself or your stride, take a step closer to Jesus. He will run to you with blessings and promises you can't imagine. Don't worry about the critics. They'll always be there. Keep your eyes on Jesus.

Joseph S. Girdler, D.Min.

Foreword

Since I was a child the one thing my parents instilled in me other than my relationship with Jesus and love for people was to do everything with a spirit of excellence. They taught me to pray over what I was doing, research it, set and manage my expectations, plan, execute, and most importantly, learn from my mistakes and give all the credit and glory to God. My wife, Tristan, always says, "Whatever we do, do it well, and do it with excellence." Just when I couldn't be held more accountable or encouraged, my five-year-old son, Jensen, will ask his one question about everything I do in life and as a pastor: "Why?"

Why do we show up for church early? Why do we meet with leaders? Why do we take our time and focus on little and big things? Why do we care about the lights, the room temperature, transitions, first impressions, hitting the gym, having a positive social media presence? No, he hasn't actually asked quite all those things, but his question of "Why?" causes me to think about why we use our words wisely, and why we work to find ourselves prepared in every sense of the word. Why? We do it because we are setting the atmosphere for the Holy Spirit to work, move, mold, and minister!

There are certain things we know to be true in life—Jesus and the Resurrection, death and taxes. If you're in ministry, you know that everything takes longer and is more expensive, but the other thing ministers know is that we can't fix anyone, and we can't save anyone, but we *can* serve, lead, and give it our all to make sure we provide a place that is inviting to people and welcoming for the Spirit to dwell.

Whether you are holding a mid-week service and removing potential distractions by planning who will be holding the microphone, walking the church through a name change in order to communicate the same message through a new method, or investing in yourself to know the difference between a boss and a leader, you are building an atmosphere for your ministry to be effective with successful results. Pastor Joe continues to be spot on with his words in *Setting the Atmosphere for the Day of Worship - II*, in addressing these vital matters!

Setting the Atmosphere for the Day of Worship, I & II are key resources to anyone looking to build a successful and healthy environment for their church. I had the privilege of moving to Kentucky nearly three years ago from the Chicago area, and within that time the Lord has grown our church from 60 to 500 people. We have seen over 250 people accept Christ, we have fed over 1,000 families, we have baptized many, launched numerous ministries, built a staff from three to twenty, increased our yearly budget by over 200 percent, and led over $600,000.00 worth of renovations. All of these things could only be done because of

1. prayer (lots of it),
2. favor from the Lord,
3. setting the atmosphere, and
4. patient and proactive leadership!

You know how to pray and ask of God, but keep in mind we as leaders have a responsibility to act, bringing change and evaluating settings, while understanding clearly what we are communicating and how we are doing it.

Remember, you are in the field of life. You can't just lead from behind a desk or through email. You've got to live the atmosphere, face the problems, and experience the church the way people do! From the time they get out of the car at church to the time they get back in, you have got to fully engage the logistics. (You don't have to know everything, but always be able to speak to your business). The smells, faces, carpet, bathrooms, tradition that doesn't make sense anymore, as well as the person who always has the mic but shouldn't—all these things, whether positive or negative, in hindsight, need to have this question posed about them, "What are you doing?" In doing so, you become self-aware and build the atmosphere for a community where people will come on their day off and serve for free because they believe in the church vision, they give 10 percent of their finances or more, and are encouraged to invite people to do the same! When you think about it, that's a tall order for unbelievers and believers alike, yet Pastor Joe not only provides pragmatic solutions, but addresses the whos, whats, hows, wheres and whys of setting the atmosphere and how doing so is vital in every ministry and local church.

As you read this, perhaps you feel overwhelmed by how many things are going wrong in the office and in the church. Maybe you're young and "green" or the opposite—seasoned and sharp. Maybe you've decided there is too much to do.

Where do you start? You may be saying, "Can I really change things around? This is all so overwhelming!" Let me encourage you as someone once encouraged me.

Regardless of what is going on in your life, you are the person for this season at your church, and the fight is not over. You have purpose, you have reason, and you are blessed beyond measure. The end of the Good Book has been written, Jesus has won, you fight for a Winner, and you have been called to this place and this time knowing well that He could have called someone else. But He didn't. He called you. Pray fervently, ask for favor, set atmosphere, and lead from behind! A good report is just around the corner. You can do this!

Be Blessed,
Ryan Franks
Lead Pastor, Journey Church, Brandenburg, KY
U-40 Director, Kentucky Assemblies of God

Introduction

Innumerable men and women serve God's Church in every region of the world. About such work, someone once said, "Missions is not crossing the sea. Missions is seeing the Cross." To that end, I write this book—that someone might see the Cross. I love the Church. I love those given to ministry. Ministers give, serve, strive, pray, and pour out daily, often for little recognition or compensation, all to get up the next day and do it all over again. Nothing gives them more pleasure than making a difference for others in light of the call of God upon their lives. They are committed to their art and see their work as a holy calling—not one they have to do, but one they get to do—and most of them love it.

I entered university with dreams of going to medical school and spending all my spare time playing jazz. Not long after, I realized medicine wasn't my cup of tea. To be honest, I hadn't learned in high school how to genuinely give energy to scholarship, and the rigors required for a career in medicine weren't anything I was interested in taking on at that juncture. The Lord saw fit to permit me falling in love with my college girlfriend, who became an esteemed physician. We had two amazing kids! Later, my son, with a smile that lights up a room, attained a college degree in religion. Many thought he was following in my footsteps, but then he applied to medical school. A guy with a religion degree applying to med school—who would have thought? Now, he and likewise my remarkable daughter-in-law live for others by service through medicine.

My second child, my daughter, is as independent a thinker as ever was born. She is full of life, loves being on the go, and brings peace with her when she walks into a room. You certainly don't want to argue politics with her; she'll win every time. And, she's quite the biblical scholar. I'm a blessed man. She grins when she reminds the family that she's "the favorite." She, too, took a similar journey of serving others, by following a career path that led to a Masters in Social Work. Today she serves in a remarkable ministry through missions in the jungles of South America. Oh, what a life we live! Though my university days were filled with jazz, we make a different kind of music now as a family.

The earlier years are not forgotten, though it was a season of my life relatively unknown to my children. The enjoyment of my music in college lasted for a season, playing small jazz ensemble gigs here and there and by generally giving countless hours to our university's over 300-member-strong marching band. The glory of those efforts was found in free tickets, bus rides, and flights to follow the University of Kentucky basketball or football teams to various SEC conference and tournament games or bowl games across the USA. But, again, I realized soon the chance of making a career out of my musical propensities was remote, particularly after devoting four university years alongside some of the most gifted instrumentalists, troubadours, songwriters, and soloists I had ever known and who as session players performed circles around me without effort. It came as no surprise to me that a few of them did go on to acclaimed music careers.

Music led me to leading worship, which led me initially to serving in such roles. Within eighteen months of my first full-time ministry position, I was tapped to serve as the church's Interim Pastor. Within two years later, I was asked to serve a second time as Interim Pastor. This led me to the pastorate and as they say, the rest is history.

God's plan for me as finally revealed was to give my life to the Church and her people. Today, I'm passionate to resource and train the next generations of her leaders.

> *Finding your own niche and the pertinent calling(s) of God on your life is key to building a great church.*

Finding your own niche and the pertinent calling(s) of God on your life is key to building a great church. You cannot simply imitate the church or the pastor down the street. Find out who you are, understand where you are, and determine how you are to impact God's kingdom and then, stay focused.

You may or may not agree with everything I write, but I'm convinced this read will challenge your thinking on a number of topics and strengthen your work for God. If you want maximum impact, read this book alongside its companion guide, the first book in the series, *Setting the Atmosphere for the Day of Worship,* also available in Spanish. The two books side-by-side go in tandem; together they form foundational guidelines for the local church and her leaders.

I love the Church, and I love her leaders. Jacob served seven years for Rachel, and they seemed but a few days because of the love he had for her (see Genesis 29:20). This story depicts how I feel about the over three decades my wife, Renee, and I have been privileged to serve the Church. I've had some ups and some downs in those years. I likely caused most of the downs, and clearly amazing team members around me helped me attain and enjoy the ups. I have seen churches grow, and I've witnessed people leave churches—or her leaders—in droves. I've dealt with struggles and headaches, and I've seen joy and happiness of mountaintop moments. Life is quite simply that—highs and lows, ups and downs, step-by-step, journey-by-journey, experience-to-experience, precept upon precept, etc. Joy comes when you can find your comfort spot through it all.

Throughout life, we all have our comfort spots. One of my comfort spots is coffee. When it comes to coffee, some prefer Starbucks' Guatemala Antigua, Komodo Dragon, a Sumatra or Café Verona; others like Peet's, Intelligentsia, Dunkin', or Caribou. At this moment, I'm sitting in my go-to Starbucks in Springfield, Missouri watching the buzz of life. My daughter, who presently lives in Costa Rica, has mentioned to me often that she regularly finds herself at her own comfort spot coffee shop in San José. We all have our preferences for whatever reasons. People are drawn to their special spot time and again. My hope is that you will likewise find your spiritual comfort-spot where you'll be drawn week to week—or, that we as global church leaders will help others find that special place for themselves; those who have found little or nothing in today's Church to draw them or persuade them to meet and grow in their knowledge of Christ. Further, this book offers some defining moments and focused clarity for church leaders to process how you are fairing in what you may think you're called to do.

As I grew in my own relationship with the Lord, I absorbed the reality that the enemy wanted nothing more than to thwart the plans God had for me. Keep in mind I've never been one to look for a devil under every rock. As a matter of fact, people who seem to do that have always caused me alarm. I definitely saw, however, ebbs and flows of how the enemy wanted to catch me off guard, tempt me at my lowest moments, or keep me from being energized in the Word or by my testimony. I also cherished knowing that Satan has no weapon that can pierce the leader whose heart is steadfast in righteousness. Therein is the question—figuring out how to walk genuinely and keep a heart of righteousness. I have deep respect to the hymnist, John Newton's lyrics: "Be thou my shield and hiding place, that sheltered near thy side, I may my fierce accuser face, and tell him thou hast died." The devil is always trying to deflate your will, destroy your dreams, and tear down whatever you have built for the Lord. If he can trip you up with the cares of the world, he can weaken your influence and lead others away from the foot of the cross, but be encouraged, friends. For those who stay true to the promises of God, steady in the journey to and beyond the Cross, humbly lifting up the name of Jesus, trusting the steps of righteous men and women ordered of the Lord, there is nothing the world or the enemy can do to take away God's promises from you. You win! Sow good seeds. I heard it said once, "The fruit you bear depends on the seeds you sow."

There are times those seeds come with challenges. Missionary Noel Perkin once said, "Some of the greatest pioneers have been the greatest sufferers." Perkin went to Argentina as a missionary at age twenty-five. Nine years later he became the Executive Director of World Missions for the Assemblies of God and a strong proponent of indigenous principles for the mission field. Suffering in the work of God is apparently not just something today's leaders have to deal with themselves. Such realities have been around from the beginning. Keep in mind, though, that freedom is available for all in the midst of a suffering church or a suffering world in need of Jesus, our Healer, our Savior, and our Hope. Hope, healing, and salvation is found no one else but Jesus Christ the Lord, and true freedom is available to all who believe.

In that hope and healing true freedom is found. Those challenges holding us hostage and weighting us down are released in Christ. "My chains fell off, my heart was free, I rose, went forth, and followed thee." Those are the words of Charles, the high-volume, heart-changed, hymn writing, brother of the great John Wesley. I have a sense he had experienced that intense glow to which others later spoke. "It's not in the great numbers of missionaries that the evangelism of the world lies, but in the intense glow with which the firebrands burn," said Oren Munger, 1945 missionary to Nicaragua. That intensity is what I've longed to see, have, hold, and exemplify in my journey with the Lord. Life is a marathon; I determined that long ago. I am on a journey, and little by little, day by day, year to year, I am running the race set before me. Sometimes I win, and other days I falter, but I'm convinced if I stay the course, the Lord will help me make a path that my family, friends, and the Church can stand upon until that great day of the Lord when we marvel at His return.

We live in a world that has become shallow in honest, candid, authentic, and respectfully straightforward truth. I find there is a searching again, in this growingly liberal post-Christian mindset of society, of truth seekers probing for voices that will speak truth in love. I want to be one of those voices. I wasn't one of the most talented or gifted orators. I didn't personally feel I had a "Hollywood" voice or talent that was magnetic or exceedingly drawing. I didn't have ... this ... or that ... but, what I did have was love, and I had a lot of it to give. So, I gave it freely to the Father and the Church, and to all who would receive as I offered that love to them and theirs for the glory of the Lord.

What I'm trying to say is (while I'm a blessed man in so many ways, and I know I am) I soon came to realize that I have nothing, and am nothing but needy.

William Cowper penned these words in 1772: "There is a fountain filled with blood, drawn from Immanuel's veins; and sinners plunged beneath that flood, lose all their guilty stains. The dying thief rejoiced to see that fountain in his day; and there have I, as vile as he, washed all my sins away." These words were clearly taken from New Testament passages such as Ephesians 1:7; 2:13; John 19:34; Colossians 1:20; and Hebrews 9:12-14, as well as Old Testament passages like Zechariah 13:1 and more. Cowper's sins were washed away. He found he was needy. What a powerful truth.

As I'm adding this paragraph, I'm sitting outside just under a small awning listening to the gentle rain, steady and refreshing. It's now Easter eve, and my wife and I are in deep eastern Kentucky at my mother-in-law's family home nestled in a genuine Kentucky hollow (or "Holler" as the locals call it) consisting of one street with homes on both sides of the road until it dead ends at the base of a cliff. Steep hills rise on both sides of the simple road behind each home. I think of tomorrow's Easter service in the small rural community church that my father-in-law planted fifty years ago.

During the magnificent Easter season, I am drawn to the memory offered today's Church of the crucified criminal dying beside Jesus. What a day it would have been to have witnessed, to have seen this man Barabbas deserving death in his final moments before eternity discern and receive the saving grace of Christ hanging beside him on that cruel tree of death; what a powerful triumph over tragedy. He brought Christ nothing but his need of a Savior, and all he offered was faith. When I was in need of that personal relationship with the Savior, far beyond the day-to-day routine of an "I go to church," and a "Sure, I believe" kind of faith, I found the promise given in Christ to be refreshing, cleansing, strengthening, and renewing. He was all I needed. His glory was revealed, and my trust was resting in Him. As Corrie Ten Boom said, "Never be afraid to trust an unknown future to a known God."

Remember friends, when His glory rests upon your life, you won't have to announce it, reveal it, produce a business card, or tell anyone. They will already know. May we seek, find, and walk in His glory revealed. In the journey, love God, love people, have a clear message, and expect God to use you in making a kingdom difference.

I've penned this sequel to *Setting the Atmosphere for the Day of Worship* to dig a little deeper, go a little farther, and to answer more of the real-world issues facing today's Church and her leaders. I've had these topics addressed to me as questions many times in my years of ministry. This easy guide is not intended as an encyclopedia of the topics, nor in any way a full-scope research on the subjects found. The topics you'll process in the pages ahead are this time (as opposed to the style of my initial book, *Setting the Atmosphere for the Day of Worship*) written in a more customary manuscript etiquette, rather than bullet-point suggestions. This book's topics are purposefully mixed and random since I found through the years of ministry every year, every month, every day, sometimes hour by hour of a day, that I never really knew what was going to be presented to me. Every day was a new adventure. Every phone call brought a new challenge. Every conversation potentially set the pace for something exciting or challenging. There were times I questioned whether it was the Lord or the devil himself who presented the schedule. Either way, I found myself loving the work of God and the people of God more and more, year after year. It is a privilege to be about the Father's business. As said before, we don't have to do this, today, this week, this month, or this year. For those of us who have been called and have chosen the journey of vocational ministry, remember—we don't have to do this, but we get to. It remains the honor of a lifetime to serve the Lord in this great harvest.

Let's begin.

Holding the Microphone

The elderly saint was naïve to the comment she made, but as it came out, more than one in the audience heard the same thing, "...and, the devil's been after me all week long, bless his holy name..." WHAT? Was that heard correctly? Oh my! There's nothing in the devil's name that is holy, and nothing to bless! Of course, that was not what she meant at all, and everyone knew that. With my smile and a bit of a sheepish grin, I could only hope she'd not go on too much longer. Still, the microphone had echoed across the church, and there was no retracting the words. Similar to this actual event, there are times the pastor or other leader will learn the hard way that microphones are not to be handed out freely to an attendee willing to talk openly when given the opportunity, or handed over to even the most sincere of saints when it's not fully known what will be coming out of his or her mouth. This simple lesson learned can help church leaders set the atmosphere for genuine God encounters for those desperately hoping to find a place of worship they feel they can trust and embrace.

When pastoring a local congregation a number of years ago, it worked well for me to incorporate occasion for members and congregants to personally share their stories, give their "testimonies" (as it was called in those days), adding more of an individual element to the service. The interactive element of church services is often missed in today's "instant" society and "planning-center" timed schedules. In my early years of pastoring, the Sunday evening service was a much more common event, and I would use that gathering and our mid-week gathering for just such personal moments. These times became a meaningful part of our liturgy. Why not offer it as a planned part of your dynamic? You might be surprised at how the Lord uses people to encourage and strengthen others. Is that not what we're to be doing, building up the church to minister one to another? Further, you will no doubt be surprised at how this simple addition to your structure will knit the body of Christ together and further develop unity throughout the church.

I've written about unity before in *Redemptive Missiology in Pneumatic Context: Practical Missions Led by the Holy Spirit*, but one can never say enough about the importance of unity in the body. In early 2019, I led a Day of Prayer held in Paducah, Kentucky for a group of about thirty ministers. In that gathering, I gave opportunity for others to lead, pray, and share personally. As one pastor began to pray, I was drawn to his passionate words, "Father, unity is good, but harmony is better, where gifts become weapons, and where a victory cry echoes through the nations..." as he continued. The individual praying was a youth pastor at the same time as was I in our fellowship in the late 1980s. Today, he is a passionate voice for God's work, and it was clear in his prayers, which energized and focused the entire group gathered. When you allow others in your meetings to become a part of your worship structure, you too will find God using them and their voice to encourage His faithful followers and challenge those who seek.

Let me offer this piece of advice to pastors and leaders when it comes to the particular moments when you need to lead, but you do want to share the microphone with others. In those instances—usually within the middle of the service—hold on to the microphone at all times. As you offer it to someone to share a word, or offer a "testimony," simply hold the microphone and lean it toward their mouths for them to speak into. They will naturally reach to take it. If you release it, there's no guarantee you'll easily get it back, and when you do get the microphone back in your hand, it might just be too late. Whatever they've said has already been said at that point. If you'll hold the microphone ever so effortlessly, yet with a bit of a sturdy grip, when they reach for it they'll sense and feel the tension and likely pull back from trying to take it out of your hand. If they do not and begin to tug with you for control of the microphone (and, that's happened more than once to me in the past), do not let it go. Smile brightly at them and let them know, and everyone else in the congregation also, that the pastor is well in control and will safely protect the flock from fear of the unknown. While you may experience that one person who will continue tugging on the microphone, I have found most congregants desire pastoral leadership that shows respectful control rather than the free-for-all and far-to-loose anything-goes approach—an environment in which anything can happen. Trust me. I speak from experience. Let your families be confident in your leadership. If something is out of hand or not done decently and in order, you will previously have given them plenty of the trust factor based on the knowledge that you will be a courageous leader and protect the saints and the work of the Lord.

Further, sometimes good people mean well, but they simply go on and on and on, and their story never seems to end. You sense people getting uncomfortable, but if you've released the microphone it's difficult to reach into their hands and take it back, cutting them off clearly before they're done, and doing it all in front of a live audience watching how they perceive you treating others. I've said before, perception is reality to the people who have it. And, if it appears that the pastor or leader is cutting people off, being rude, or whatever the case may be, that will be a challenge to overcome. The best thing is to not find oneself in that circumstance in the first place. Hold the microphone in those specific moments of which I speak. Don't let go of it, even if you know and trust the source. Do it all with a smile. Simultaneously, you will be serving as a courageous and loving pastor to your flock. This chapter is not as much about who is holding a microphone as it is

> *Let your families be confident in your leadership.*

setting a standard of excellence and a precedent of pastoral protection, covering, and leadership.

Certainly, there are times when exceptions can and should be made, but they are rare. Lead discerningly. Let the Holy Spirit guide you. Listen attentively as He speaks.

Chapter 2

Polishing Your Shoes

What does this have to do with *Setting the Atmosphere for the Day of Worship*? First, let's keep in mind whose "day of worship" we could be speaking about. Communities are filled with good people who have given little interest to the things of God, the house of the Lord, the local church, or the efforts of community ministries. I know many people who have not stepped foot inside a church building in years. Others only have been inside once in their entire lives. Yet others have never in their lifetime walked inside a place of worship. When the Spirit draws them to do so, they should find ample reason to trust what they hear, what they sense, what they see, and what they seek.

I've heard it said that the first thing people look at when they encounter someone, dressed for whatever the occasion, is their shoes. Oddly, I've noticed through the years, I seem to do the same, immediately noticing the banker's shoes, the D-1 basketball player's shoes, the Starbucks employee's shoes, the mechanic's shoes, my physician's shoes, the nurse's shoes, the engineer's shoes, the professor's shoes, ... and yes ... the pastor, priest, preacher, or minister's ...shoes.

You may think it odd, but I've actually been amazed at the number of times I've met pastors and noticed how unkempt their appearance seemed. Let's face facts. I too have had my days when I'm just not on game. Maybe it's a season of weight gain, or I'm just simply tired and not taking that good care of myself. Too often, however, today's relaxed culture brushes an unkempt appearance off with the excuse, "That's just me," or, "I prefer the natural approach." Sometimes I sense a careless attitude from a person's actions or personality traits, and other times it's perceivable from the way he or she is dressed; quite simply the wear, smeared dirt, mud (yes, mud), and scuffs of their shoes that haven't been polished in months—or possibly ever—tell the story. To a guest at church, such an appearance makes a bad first impression and sends the message that rather than the leader and trusted shepherd of the flock they had hoped to see and meet, the pastor is likely a shuffled newcomer to the business, or a long-termer who honestly just shouldn't be in that position any longer and who needs a good bit of polishing him or herself.

Shoes communicate. However, I'm not solely speaking of shoes. Sometimes, the shoes I've just described—unbeknownst to the ministers wearing them of course—communicate that their ministry is possibly just as unkempt as the shoes they're sporting. I've said before, "Perception is reality to the people who have it."

In the early 1980s when I was attending college and churches and church leaders around me were molding my spiritual life, it was common to see the worship service "uniform." Both male and female leaders wore clothing that communicated the credibility, esteem, and accountability of the leader. For men, a dark, two-piece suit was acceptable attire with a conservative white shirt and slightly personality-driven accompanying tie.

Their ministry is possibly just as unkempt as the shoes they're sporting.

Hopefully the tip of the tie fell just at the top of the belt buckle and did not land embarrassingly at mid-drift. I saw that again recently and thought to myself, "Should I say something?" Or, "Should I volunteer to go to a back room and re-tie his tie for him?" I opted to not offer shallow words and keep quiet. For women leaders of the 1980s, the worship service "uniform" usually included neutral colors, varying fabrics, but few embellishments, teased hair, big hats, big handbags, and big shoulders. While fluctuating or changeable skirts or neckline styles existed, modesty often reigned (based on generational demographics) with maxi or embroidered long-sleeve midi dresses. The point is that there was seemingly an acceptable standard of leadership modesty that communicated trust and credible influence. This holds true today.

I recall a trusted ministry colleague mentioning to me years ago when I commented about how pristine his shoes appeared (he was dressed like a professional, which he was), that the shoes he was wearing "were just for Sunday." He wore them only to "the day of worship," to offer his best, and present his best to the Lord and the Lord's people to whom he would minister that day. That made an impression on me that I well remember to this day. Since that day, I've kept a new pair of shoes boxed and in my closet that I only take out or put on occasionally.

Often in our North American context people will laugh at the numbers of shoes women have in their closets. I know that some men also have (in my opinion) an exorbitant collection of shoes, too. How many times has my beautiful bride in our thirty-plus years together, walked into a room and said, "Do these shoes go with this outfit?" Or, "What do you think of this look?" Again, the point remains as noted from those examples, it matters to offer one's best when placed in positions of public leadership. It also encourages the leaders to stand a little taller and lead a little stronger when they're aware that their appearance is well tuned.

Well, maybe there's something to presenting our best, being our best, offering to the Lord our best—whatever that may be. Even with cultural variances as to attire and platform protocols in the present day, I suggest that ministers of the gospel consider at the very least polishing their shoes. And, by now, you hopefully realize I may not be solely (Don't you just love that metaphor?) speaking of … shoes. Leaders should be more cognizant of what they portray, both in appearance and ministry.

Leading Board Meetings

I never cease to be amazed at the numbers of pastors and church leaders who seem to find time for everything except board meetings, elders' meetings, or staff meetings. One certain way to ensure that the atmosphere of your church is not adequately prepared for worshippers to fully embrace the atmosphere for worship is to leave them contemplating, guessing, curious, or even concerned. Concerned about what? It doesn't take much for people to be concerned that things aren't being handled quite right, or that integrity isn't being fully embraced behind closed doors of leadership. Too often people can see clearly that excellence in ministry is not the bar of standard. Did you read the first two chapters? Just as is in the leadership provided for a service, what is allowed to be broadcast over microphones, or through the physical or spiritual leadership portrayed by appearance and presentation, board meetings and staff meetings are likewise important.

More than one church board member over the years has told me that their pastor had not held a board meeting in over a year, maybe two years, or more. Pastors have told me that they find little need to hold a special meeting when the church's board or elders see each other every time they meet for a service and can just talk amongst themselves in the sanctuary, hallway, or parking lot. *Seriously?*

If you have ever been a part of a boring, unfulfilling, or dreadful board meeting, you've no doubt surely been tempted to raise the question, "Why have them?" If you are in a rural setting, or even in a small church setting, it's easy to suggest a quick powwow for the sake of church unity with your leaders. But keep this in mind—you owe it to your congregation to supply them with the best possible source of leadership, and holding consistent monthly—or regularly scheduled—board meetings is in my opinion the best way of doing that!

Board meetings are not held to simply crunch numbers, address financial reports, or deal with the question of who's been missing from the church. Board meetings are the meetings before the meetings. Effective leaders always walk into sessions prepared, on time, with their thoughts, agenda, and discerning radar on target for the room and the heat of the topic(s). Good leaders dream, they address stakeholders, they bounce ideas off their inner circle, they listen, they adjust, and they address! Board meetings are held to be effective, not routine or mundane. Board meetings can be used to vision cast, get the buy-in of your peers, and intentionally disclose seemingly dispassionate initiatives motivating the church for that moment when you finally come to the stage. Those moments can then help people sit on the edge of their seats. When you address the crowds, you'll already know the board is behind you, you'll know if they have discussed it to any sense with their families, that those family members are behind you, and that the church leadership has been well informed and are supportive as you move ahead.

If you ever have the opportunity to speak to the leadership of Journey Church in Brandenburg, Kentucky, you'll realize that before all the vision-casting, renovations, and growth, the seed of hope for all they've done was dropped first into the board room, with just a young pastor and three older gentlemen. The pastor said, "Will you take a chance on this?" And the older gentlemen said, "What do we have to lose?" All it takes is several willing voices to say, "Let's do this!"

Regardless of where you stack up in this conversation, I simply choose to believe the best in people. I've decided through the years that most pastoral leaders truly want to do things correctly. In some circumstances, well-meaning leaders simply may not know how to do something or how to be better at what their ministry is lacking. Having appropriate meetings and keeping minutes of them is essential. Initially, there even may be a few legal matters related to organizations keeping filed and official minutes of meetings. It is possible that without filed minutes of board meetings, the IRS or the public could call into question matters of compliance related to following bylaws, or they could take issue pertaining to board participation among nonprofit law and compliance regulations.

Official minutes are an important but often undervalued resource. They provide a remembered account of key information such as board activities, elections of officers or executives, and definite reports from teams and staff.

So, schedule and hold those meetings on a regular basis. What is regular? I suggest monthly, but based on each church's context, it could be quarterly or weekly, as the case may necessitate. When you meet, take minutes. Keep your minutes generic. There's no need to list, "Bro. Jones said... then Bro. Smith voted... And, the final decision was..." Have the conversation, vote as needed, and simply log, "A motion prevailed with ... or without dissenting vote (as the case may be) to..." If at all possible, type the minutes as opposed to handwriting them. For official minutes, typed is far more legible, professional, and acceptable for any who would later need to review them.

Perhaps we've introduced some details too quickly. You might ask, "What are minutes?" Legally chartered organizations function with their official notes recorded from meetings of members or trustees. It has always been my perspective that documented minutes would be considered open to all official members in good standing of the organization, but that doesn't mean that any member can or should expect to simply walk in at any time without an appointment or without announcing one's arrival, and expect to go through all the official minutes. Do all things systematically and respectfully.

Typically, a church secretary will record the minutes of a board meeting unless someone else has been appointed to serve in that role for various meetings. It would be most appropriate for the secretary to present in written form (preferably typed) the minutes to all board members prior to or at the onset of the meeting. I've seen some messy files, so my suggestion is that pages of the minutes be numbered with the date of the meeting listed appropriately. The documenting secretary should with his or her signature sign off on the conclusion of the prepared minutes for detail and accountability.

Have a board meeting agenda prepared in advance by the pastor/or acting chair of the board, and send that out to the board members prior to the meeting so they know exactly what's on the agenda prior to their arrival. This allows them to consider their opinions and thoughts accordingly. It's respectful to the members of the board and saves an enormous amount of time when the board meets together. Further, letting board members see the agenda in advance allows them to not be surprised, caught off guard (in those occasional moments that something would be such), or frustrated that they didn't know what was going on until they got there. Good leaders help avoid those potential pitfalls and set the pace for solid communication and healthy relationships through the dialogues.

Although adding to an agenda something to discuss that may not have gotten added to the pre-prepared agenda is often acceptable, it also allows the potential for misunderstandings, undue frustrations, or angst. When you send out the pre-prepared agenda prior to the meeting for members to review, respectfully allow them the opportunity to add a discussion topic they may feel is prudent for the church or ministry. Simply ask them to send that item in advance so you can add it to the agenda prior to the meeting. That also allows for due respect to you as pastor/board chair, so you don't get caught off guard. If a topic submitted needs to be discussed to some extent between the board member adding it and the pastor/board chair, then respectfully do that in advance of the meeting to talk through the heart and soul of the matter(s).

Not long after beginning a pastorate, I determined it was quite difficult to have discussions about ministry vision, ministry departments, the youth ministries, children ministries, nursery ministries, young adults, senior saints, or whatever, without me having the key leaders sitting in the room at the time, to help with understanding and to provide dialogue as questions or insights arose. While sometimes board members may want or need to speak privately without other church staff present, those times are rare if the church is healthy. If the person needs to speak with you privately, you can easily acknowledge that to the staff present, that at a pre-set arranged time on the agenda, staff relative to the issue may need to step out for a few minutes before they return (so board members can speak openly).

I found it marvelously helpful having staff present in board meetings. The unity built among the pastors on the staff and the board members as they met together as colleagues built respect for one another, and for church ministry vision, synergy, and church health. Consider adding your church ministry leaders (paid or volunteer) to your board meetings. Board/staff meetings are healthy in my opinion and experience. If you have not done this previously, but would like to in the future, be respectful to the fact that you're possibly changing a years-long culture. Don't just do it without speaking to the relevant parties involved. Bring it up first to the church board members as a part of your next month's board meeting

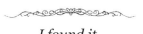

I found it marvelously helpful having staff present in board meetings.

agenda to have the discussion. That again builds trust among you and your leadership and demonstrates that you're not just a rogue leader who's going off the deep end or doing as you please without even talking about the change to the leaders who matter. Be smart. Play fair. Build trust. Live church health.

What should an agenda list? A multitude of styles exist for agendas that will work for your church. Below is a sample of some topics to get you started if your church or personal leadership initiatives suggest you do a little better in this particular systems process.

- Welcome/Devotions/Communion/Prayer
- Call to Order
- Review and Approval of Previous Meeting Minutes
- Review and Approval of Present Agenda
- Pastor's Report
- Committee Reports
- Staff Ministries Reports

- Unfinished Business
- New Business
- Adjournment/Prayer

Have you considered having food (sandwiches, finger foods, snack foods, or home-made cuisines), tea, soft drinks, and coffee (unless you opt to avoid caffeine, and if you do, that's fine; you can serve water) at your board meetings? You should. On the practical side, if you set meetings on an evening or early evening after board members have worked long days at their jobs/careers, providing food gives them the opportunity of having something to eat at the meeting itself. Beyond the practical reasons for having food, strategically, I have found that when people share a meal together, they tend to work better together, also. Jesus set that example. Why shouldn't we follow it likewise?

Board meetings are an act of spiritual worship. God-given leaders are giving of themselves to the Lord and to their church with their talents and leadership gifts to help the church be all she can be for the work of God. Consider serving Communion to your board members at the onset of the meeting. I've done this occasionally and have known friends and colleagues who've done it regularly. It builds a spiritual dynamic among the church's leadership. When dicey topics do arise, if you've just had Communion together, it makes it a little more challenging to become angry at one another. I'd like to think the stats are in my favor for avoiding conflict when the pastor has set the atmosphere for the day of worship.

Although it is not always the acceptable choice based on what you're dealing with at any given moment, taking the posture of "When in doubt, don't," is a good position to trust. For many years of board meetings, I would lead discussions, take votes on topics, and prayerfully discern whether the church should proceed, or not, with a given subject or decision. Most often when votes of the board were split or not solidly unified, as chair/pastor I would table the decision or discussion to be brought up at the next meeting for further discussion. Sometimes we'd have things on an agenda for months. Some things we'd move forward with and other things we would take off the table permanently all because I was looking for unity within our leadership on the topic. Few mountains are worth dying on. Determine which one's matter. You only live life once and one wrong verdict can thwart church health and your leadership for the remainder of its entirety

Chapter 4

Serving Eucharist, The Lord's Supper, Communion

I believe in the power of Communion, an intimate remembrance of Jesus, His death, burial, and powerful resurrection. His forgiveness of my sins and His promises for everyday life are both more than narrative to me. They are a reliable and accurate chronicle of veracity and life. The primary text for this soul-probing moment of contemplative reflection is usually 1 Corinthians 11:23-29.

While a student in Greek classes taken in seminary, I did absorb sufficient perspective to check for context and tense. The Greek uses the word *anamnesis* to describe a memorial or remembrance—in this case of Christ's redeeming death for the believer. While observing what Christ accomplished through His death is the principle reason of His command, "This do in remembrance of me" (1 Cor 11:24-25, KJV), I was recently reminded by a friend of the power in remembering the whole of Jesus's life and words. Jesus received the children. Jesus healed the blind and the sick. Jesus fed the hungry. Jesus walked on water. Jesus raised Lazarus from the dead. He performed miracles at the wedding in Cana. He humbled himself to wash people's feet. He broke all cultural norms to meet the woman at the well and the woman caught in adultery. He called the disciples. And, Jesus proclaimed himself the Bread of Life, the Light of the World, the Good Shepherd, The True Vine, and more. Jesus also commanded this personal confession for believers. It was His mandate that believers proclaim His death in this manner until His return. For unbelievers, infants, or children who do not comprehend, I definitively suggest refraining from serving them the elements of Communion. This memorial to the Cross of Jesus is a mark of Christian profession, representing mutual devotion among believers of like precious faith. 1 Corinthians 11:27 speaks of those who are not followers of Christ, who do not comprehend the personal profession and seal of the promises of His death and life partaking without regarding the worth of the commemoration. When Communion is flippantly received, individuals become guilty, treating as common that which is sacred, drinking damnation to themselves (1 Cor 11: 28-29). It is more important than most realize that partakers in the Communion service examine themselves, searching their hearts, avoiding form and ritual, applying the new covenant promises of Christ's blood to one's lives.

> *It is more important than most realize that partakers in the Communion service examine themselves.*

When you give thought to your church's Communion moments other passages that will bring strength to the service include: Psalm 139: 23-24; Matthew 26: 27-29; Mark 14:22-25; Luke 22: 19-20; Acts 2:42; and 1 Corinthians 10:16, 21. Consider having your congregation quietly and reflectively sing that timeless hymn, "The Old Rugged Cross." Make your Communion service meaningful by telling the story, explaining the characters, and using the symbols to bring the message of Christ to people seeking to know the depth of this powerful promise: Communion.

Through the years when pastoring a local church, I would offer and serve Communion in our service one week per month. Often, I would share a brief scriptural message and pray as the elements were offered to everyone. Most times, I would have a trusted friend and long-time staff member, lead the Communion service for our congregation. It was our church's system for that season. He and I had attended seminary together in the mid-1980s, and years later we were still friends and doing ministry as a team. The congregation trusted him as much as did I, and he always did an excellent job of ministering the elements and sharing a meaningful word to the congregants.

While I served our congregation the elements monthly (on periods of one Sunday per month), many churches offer Communion weekly. Whatever the frequency a church leadership may choose, the point I want to make is that I had a system. I think Jesus is more intent on the fact that we are making Communion an act of our worship and our lives, than He is with varying fellowships disagreeing on how often, in what way, or the particular format to which it is offered. As I have served at this juncture for nearly sixteen years (at this writing) as a denominational superintendent for one of the world's largest church fellowships, I travel and minister in pulpits within different cities week to week. Often, I've been puzzled and even perplexed at the numbers of pastors I find that do not offer consistent or systematic Communion opportunities for their memberships. I know of churches that have not served Communion in many years. Maybe you are gasping at this moment, but there are varying reasons for tragedies such as that. The key is, if that's you or your church, begin now to search out the reason, and pray through the depth of this Christ mandate. Then find the amazing power of Communion once again in your worship services or in your private moments visiting members unable to be in service due to being shut-in or in the hospital.

It is likewise important to keep in mind the Bible actually teaches there are reasons one should not receive Communion. Eating the bread and drinking the juice (or wine, as the case may be in some churches) in no way makes one a Christian or a genuine follower of Christ. The concept taught in the church of the saving of souls or going to heaven does not occur nor is guaranteed by such acts of receiving Communion. Salvation is received solely by repentance of sins and by God's grace (Ephesians 2:8) through faith in our personal acceptance of Jesus Christ as Lord and Savior. Paul went so far as to write to the Corinthians (1 Cor 11:27-31) that intentionality was the key when it came to Communion.

He taught that those who are believers are to purposefully consider what Jesus has completed and why He accomplished it.

When I personally led the Communion service, it was not uncommon that I would incorporate a strategic element to the segment to include the opportunity of soul searching, as was alluded to above. After the elements had been distributed and I shared a scriptural word to all in the audience, I would then make a point to respectfully but righteously acknowledge the "Search me, O God..." (Ps 139:23-24, KJV) concept; I would remind everyone, myself included, that the admonition of the Lord from 1 Corinthians 11:27 was to ensure we did not partake of the elements unworthily. In our worship structure, everyone in the audience (unless guided otherwise on occasion) would be instructed to hold the elements in their hands until all were served. Then we would partake together. While the individuals were holding the small piece of Communion bread and the small cup (we used grape juice, as our AG Fellowship holds to a strong biblical evidence for abstinence from alcohol; another topic for another time), I would offer a pastoral prayer—something like this:

> I would like us all to take a moment to search our hearts before we partake together, as Jesus Christ has asked of us. If you are here today, holding the elements in your hands, but in your heart you know you have not personally accepted Christ as your Lord and Savior, I want you to know we're glad you're here, and it's okay to be honest with yourself and with God. If you are here

knowing that you are not living for Christ in your journey, then with heads bowed, eyes closed, and hearts in prayer, you can at this moment with no guilt whatsoever simply set the elements down beside you in honor of God's holy word.

Almost every time there would be individuals who would do just that. I have found through the years, people— whether serving Christ or not—if they are sitting in church especially, are most genuine in not wanting to offend, or in any way be irreverent. Now, there are some, certainly, who could care less, but most often giving people the opportunity to show that respect to God's Word, when you've shared the word with them and they have heard it for themselves, builds a bridge of trust to them, even though they are admitting they are not believing Christians or Christ-followers.

I would then continue with a Communion prayer and quiet reflections. Then just before I invited all to partake together I would offer this promise.

Friends, just before I pray, if you happened to have set down your Communion elements a few moments ago, but at this very moment feel in your heart you do want to participate in remembering the death, burial, and resurrection of Jesus; you do acknowledge Jesus as the Savior of the world who came to live and die that His blood might be the covering for your sins, as I once received for my own... then even now... I invite you to pick back up the elements and today ... for the first time in your life... or as you are newly rededicating your life to Christ... partake of the Communion today with us, knowing you now are receiving in full acknowledgement and trust in Jesus as your Lord and Savior. I'll wait just a moment to allow you to make that personal decision right now.

I would wait during that moment promised, with music playing gently in the background, or with a special Communion song to be led in worship just before we partook together. Time and again, individuals came to me after services to tell me they had prayed that prayer that day, and had set down their Communion elements but picked them up again, just as I had offered—this time to partake for the first time in their lives as true believers.

Serving Communion to Christ-followers offers remembrance to the life-giving power of Christ. Often, people look alive on the outside but are dying on the inside. Communion's self-examination causes one to anticipate the hope offered. Most beautifully, God's renewing presence declares unity for those who believe.

Pastors and Shepherds of God's church carry the responsibility of fulfilling Christ's commands. If pastors do not offer Communion to their church's members or guests, how can they find themselves faithful to fulfill Christ's command to participate in Communion? Let's begin there. If you're serving as a pastor, it is important to follow Christ's commands. I do believe it starts with the pastor. God's shepherd of the local flock is the one to open doors, close doors, and provide the moments that change people's lives. If parishioners do not receive or partake in this scriptural admonishment, it might very well be the pastor's fault, not theirs. The act of worship within Communion is fundamental for the church as a body and for individuals as faithful and worshipful disciples. Begin now scheduling Communion service moments for your church—if not weekly, then on some systematic basis. You will be surprised how intimate and meaningful that service will become for devoted followers of Christ. I even had church attending guests give their lives to Christ during the Communion service. Don't sell that moment short. It is a powerful mandate of Christ for us to do—in remembrance of Him.

For others, there may simply be bewilderment and disconnect as to the whole concept. Does the whole notion of eating a small wafer, piece of bread, or cracker chip, and receiving a minute sip of grape juice (often) or wine (in some churches) at a church worship service, find you confused? If so, you can relax. Thousands of others are also confused as to what it all means and where the concept originated. Seriously? Yes. We, as guests in churches, need more explanations, and pastors need to recognize that not everyone understands what they or their regulars may consider standard fare. I mean, we get that "It's about remembering Jesus," but isn't everything at a church about "remembering Jesus?" What's the deal with the bread and juice?

Bread serves as an emblem for the body of Jesus Christ. The wine or juice serves as a symbol for Christ's bloodshed on the Cross for the sins of all mankind. 1 Corinthians 11:23-26 is the passage where Jesus taught devotees to receive

Communion. His sacrifice on the Cross is worthy of remembering and is a spiritual act of worship.

Remember, a number of churches, as does mine, and especially most conservative evangelical fellowships, interpret Scripture to encourage abstinence from alcohol of any kind. At one point, while I pastored a conservative, Protestant, alcohol-abstinent congregation, I had a parishioner once ask me, "Pastor, we all didn't come from the same denominational backgrounds. Why don't you just start placing real wine on the outside rims of the Communion plate and your grape juice in the center slots? You could simply let everyone know, and then whatever they're accustomed to would be offered." I

Every hope is in Jesus.

wondered if he would have wanted a Merlot, a red wine, a kosher wine, or since we were in the heart of Kentucky bourbon country, if he might be suggesting I add the Woodford Reserve (Woodford County, Kentucky, was where the church was located) Double Oaked Bourbon (90.4 Proof). For those of you who understand the Communion set concept with the individual Communion cup slots, you smile along with me, no doubt. I grinned and voiced appreciation of his gesture, but felt it might be best to stay with my standard protocol. Clearly, I knew I had a few challenges with my friend in getting him to understand what we believed in the bigger picture.

Every act of worship is for Jesus. Every hope is in Jesus. Salvation is found in no one else, for there is no other name under heaven given to humankind by which we must be saved (Acts 4:12, NIV). Always remember Christ and what He has provided. He is all we need, and He said that we do this in remembrance of Him. Pastors, offer God's people Communion.

Chapter 5

Teaching Tithing:
Holy Unto the Lord And The
Accountability of Finances

The matter of tithing is critically important in today's church. Further, not nearly enough respect is given to the context of accountability in finances. In the next several pages we will address these most important topics for today's Church and her leaders. Let's begin with accountability.

Accountability

Accountability in finances has been imperative for centuries. Unfortunately, more than once through the years I've been privy to churches having to deal with unscrupulous treasurers, skimming the accounts to the multiplied thousands of dollars before anyone notices. It never ends well.

Consider these passages from the New Testament: "If then you have not been faithful in the unrighteous wealth, who will entrust to you the true riches?" (Luke 16:11, ESV).

"Moreover, it is required in stewards that a man be found faithful" (1 Cor 4:2, KJV). Or, from the Old Testament, "Abram said to the king of Sodom, I have lifted my hand to the Lord, God Most High, Possessor of heaven and earth, that I would not take a thread or a sandal strap or anything that is yours, lest you should say..." (Gen 14:22-23, ESV). A trustworthy guardian considers these basic foundations for financial accountability. Such a one will spend prudently, circumvent debt, obtain counsel, give liberally, invest meticulously, and be dedicated to coaching the entire church—from children to senior adults—to do likewise.

Debt is slavery. As Proverbs says, "The borrower is servant to the lender" (22:7, NIV). Saving when you can and saving as much as you can is wise for any individual or corporation. *The Living Bible* phrases it this way: "The wise man saves for the future, but the foolish man spends whatever he gets" (Prov 21:20, TLB). "Steady plodding brings prosperity; hasty speculation brings poverty" (21:5, TLB).

This chapter is not designed to be all-encompassing to the topics of financial or fiscal structure, but rather to encourage church leaders in due diligence and to carefully examine how they process their finances. First, it is prudent to have two counters for all offerings received at the church or in services), to have clearly-understood and detailed count sheets signed by all counters, to have two signers on checks when possible, and

> *You can't have too much accountability.*

to make sure you have protections and firewalls in every arena. Everything you do is for the safety of the individuals you have performing these functions and for the church or organization's integrity within the public arena you serve. You can't have too much accountability.

Tithing

Let's look at a few topics on tithing, money, and giving. Jesus taught more on finances that any other topic in the Bible, so clearly it was an important topic to Him and one He felt was critical to teach and disciple those who would follow. Here's where I determined in studying God's Word that giving was a scriptural principle. I'll let you make up your own mind, of course, and would never force my faith or beliefs on another person. But, I certainly don't mind admitting, I have no problem with sharing with you my faith and encouraging you to search out God's truth for yourself. The Bible says, "Ask, and it shall be given you; seek, and ye shall find; knock, and it shall be opened unto you..." (Matt 7:7, KJV). So, ask, seek, and knock. I'm convinced Jesus will hear your heart and answer the genuine and searching soul for truth.

What about tithing? If one speaks of finances and spiritual financial accountability, they must also address the biblical concept of tithing. First, I encourage you to be a tither. Second, I encourage pastors to be faithful in their tithe. Third, I encourage pastors to be aware of who tithes and who gives to the church. And, yes, there's a difference between general giving of offerings and actual biblical tithing.

I hear varying discussions from time to time about whether or not a pastor should be aware of the tithers in his or her church. Some say, "No, I don't want to be distracted by those things." Others say, "I don't want to know because I don't want to treat anyone differently." Others mused, "I should stay to the spiritual things and leave the fiscal things to someone else." And, I've heard others say, "Money and tithing is personal and none of my business what people feel they should or should not do."

Well, that's okay. We can agree to disagree. I am more a member of the camp that would rather say, "Pastors are shepherds, and they should know the sheep of their pastures. As such, that means growing disciples of Jesus (our ultimate goal) in every walk of one's life." Seriously, had someone not taught me from Scripture that tithing was a biblical principle promised for God's blessings when cheerfully given, and actually showed it to me in God's Word, I would likely not be a tither today. My life through the years I was raising my family to date, my children in their own right and their now-adult lives, and my wife in her individual career journey, as well, have been blessed beyond measure. I don't want to think about what I could have missed in the spiritual realm had Renee and I not committed to tithing when we first married. Yes, it wasn't easy to tithe, especially when there was little in the checkbook (that's the old fashioned way people used to deal with economy—a checkbook), but the walk of faith is amazing when you see Jesus do His marvelous works in your life. One's faith in and faithfulness to God's biblical principles of tithing brings a tangible understanding to, "Taste and see that the Lord is good" (Ps 34:8, KJV).

Pastor Ryan Franks once shared with me what he felt college had not prepared him for. He said "Pastor, I can dissect the Bible, interpret it, offer homiletics and hermeneutics, I can sing, play guitar, and play drums. I'm quite appealing on paper. But I felt I didn't well know how to become debt-free with my finances, run a small business, use Word, Excel spreadsheets, do my taxes, or set a church budget! I had to learn that all on my own. If financial leaders had not taught me the ropes, I would have drowned because I didn't understand business or money!"

You have to budget; know how much is coming in and how much is going out! There are no lead pastors worth mentioning who aren't great business leaders, as well. Learn to speak to your business, address budgets, stick to budgets, and plan for the future. Too many churches do not have yearly budgets. That's insane. At the end of the day, not having an annual budget is acting in an unreliable, irresponsible, and possibly even unbiblical manner in every sense of the word.

The Bible speaks of the tithe being a tenth, and holy.

The Bible speaks of the tithe being a tenth, and holy. "And concerning the tithe of the herd, or of the flock, even of whatsoever passeth under the rod, the tenth shall be holy unto the LORD" (Lev 27:32, KJV). "Honor the Lord with your wealth and with the firstfruits of all your produce; then your barns will be filled with plenty... (Prov 3:9-10, ESV). From this, I learned that a genuine biblical tithe was from the gross, not the net. Malachi 3:8-12 speaks of a number of tithing truths—from defrauding or robbing God from that which was holy and to be His, to the topic of where the tithe should be given or sent, to the fact that God will pour out blessings on those who faithfully follow His word:

> 8Will a man rob God? Yet you are robbing me. But you say, 'How have we robbed you?' In your tithes and contributions. 9You are cursed with a curse, for you are robbing me, the whole nation of you. 10Bring the full tithe into the storehouse, that there may be food in my house. And thereby put me to the test, says the Lord of hosts, if I will not open the windows of heaven for you and pour down for you a blessing until there is no more need. 11I will rebuke the devourer for you, so that it will not destroy the fruits of your soil, and your vine in the field shall not fail to bear, says the Lord of hosts. 12Then all nations will call you blessed, for you will be a land of delight, says the Lord of hosts (Mal 3:8-12, ESV).

So, if every man and woman is to bring their tithe to the storehouse, what is a storehouse? The storehouse is the local church or spiritual covering where you are fed and ministered spiritual truth. If there is a need in your home, who do you call? The local pastor who loves and prays for you and your family is the one most people would call, providing they have a pastor of faith and trust, integrity and virtue.

Beyond these basics the Bible goes on to explain that blessings come from God. "Every good gift and every perfect gift is from above, coming down from the Father of lights, with whom there is no variation or shadow due to change" (James 1:17, ESV). Those blessings from God should be acknowledged back to Him in our worship and with gratitude. He sees everything in our lives anyway. Thus, I encourage people to give faithfully and thank God for the faith to do so. Hebrews 4:13 (ESV) says, "And no creature is hidden from his sight, but all are naked and exposed to the eyes of him to whom we must give account." The Bible teaches us that everything is all God's anyway. We give back to Him what is already His: "But who am I, and what is my people, that we should be able thus to offer willingly? For all things come from you, and of your own have we given you." (1 Chron 29:14, ESV). The same passage teaches that God blessed Israel because they gave willingly.

In the New Testament Paul wrote to the Corinthians about the principle of sowing and reaping, and the people gave cheerfully. I've learned through the years that we reap more than we sow. God's returns are in multiple form.

> 6The point is this: whoever sows sparingly will also reap sparingly, and whoever sows bountifully will also reap bountifully. 7Each one must give as he has decided in his heart, not reluctantly or under compulsion, for God loves a cheerful giver. 8And God is able to make all grace abound to you, so that having all sufficiency in all things at all times, you may abound in every good work" (2 Cor 9:6-8, ESV).

If leaders are not tithing, then how can they expect to teach others in good faith, with integrity, that tithing is a biblical principle and an expected norm for members of God's church? If a pastor or church board member doesn't tithe, how can he or she receive tithes and offerings from congregants with a good conscience? I don't know, but unfortunately it's done week after week, in city after city, without anyone even giving it a second thought. That's just wrong on so many levels.

God's returns are in multiple form.

One time a church finance officer was dismissed for not tithing. The leader was respected, professional in his finance career, held a graduate degree from a prestigious American seminary, and was a trusted friend to the pastor. It was determined that the tithing faithfulness was lack when it came to this key church leader. (Tithing was a church standard, biblical principle, and requirement for actual membership in the local church). To this day, the pastor well remembers the restaurant where he sat down for a private lunch with the leader (also a church board member) and was politely informed (though the conversation quickly turned uncomfortable) that "in prayer the Lord had said it was okay to use their family's tithe money to help the gentleman's spouse (who'd been struggling with emotional things) to buy new clothes and material things to encourage, love, and bless her." After all, God loves and cares for the least of things in our lives. Surely, the pastor should/would understand that, as he too loved his wife with all his heart.

The pastor took one bite of food, and the rest was left on the plate, as quickly into the meeting he had lost his appetite.

Yes, the leader was informed immediately he was relieved of his duties and that the pastor no longer had need of his services. What would the pastor do to cover for this man's service? He didn't know, but he knew his integrity was now on the line. He knew he'd been pushed to a limit that he would not and could not cross. He knew a power struggle was now ensuing, and it wasn't between himself and a financial advisor. It was spiritual. He was convinced he could not let the devil win that battle. He had always committed to himself and to the Lord that he would lead courageously if put in a position where he had to react, so he did. The church survived. God was honored, and the church soon thrived. The pastor, leaders, and membership (who were never told the story, of course, for integrity), who on their own started to put two and two together did realize they had a young pastor who would apparently stand his ground for what he believed to be spiritual and biblical principles.

When I pastored a church, I had a process for looking at tithe reports of our membership and leaders. Now, this may or may not be what you would choose to do, or how you would opt to approach this at-times-dicey subject, but it worked for me. If this is something that would work for you, then use it. If not, move on. I simply want you to be as efficient and effective for the Lord as you can possibly be, and finances are critical to the work of the Lord and the hearts of His people. So, here's how it worked for me. As pastor, I didn't regularly give detail to knowing the financial contributions of any given individual or family in our church. Still, with that said, the topic of tithing was an important and spiritual element of our church. It was listed in discussion, sermon planning, and expectancies for actual members of the church, certainly and especially for leadership. Something included in almost every public service, the receiving of tithes and offerings, was viewed as an act of worship. So, clearly it was a significant part of our church (as is most).

There are many ways beyond finances that God's people serve and give to the Lord and His Church. But, usually twice a year, I would preach a message specifically on money, tithing, and giving one's finances to the Lord and His work. So, it was in our culture and remains in my theological DNA as a scripturally based principle that I genuinely believe every believer in Jesus Christ should follow.

About once a year, I would go to our church bookkeeper and tell her in advance that "next month I will ask you for a printed copy of the giving statement for our church's staff, board members, and other leaders, as to their tithes and offerings." Those things were kept week to week, of course, as we would send annual giving statements at the end of the year to all donors. I would then at the monthly staff and board meeting inform our leaders, "Next month, I will review a printout of my own and of each of our giving statements to the church and ministries, since we are the leaders of the church, and it is vitally important that we have full integrity as leaders to be faithful to what we ask our congregants to do when it comes to giving." I would tell our leaders, "If by chance your tithes or giving are not up to date, or there's something there that for some reason you would be hard pressed to explain, then certainly do know that (1) this confidential information is for my eyes only and yours, (2) this is only an accountability follow-up once a year because "to whom much is given, much is required," and (3) I'm giving us all a month to make sure things are in order, because I would in no way want to embarrass anyone or place you in a compromising situation by discovering something that didn't make sense for a leader." Giving them that month offered some time for them to be aware in advance and take care of anything they wanted to, without my having seen any reports. Then, I would explain to them (4) if any of them wanted to speak with me privately between now and then, they could contact me. We would then have a trusted, friendly discussion if there was anything they needed to explain or if there was any way I could offer my support to them in a trying time. After all, our leaders were amazing people, trusted colleagues and friends, and as their pastor I did authentically love and care for them—whether something was amiss or not. I found this approach dependable and honorable, and so did they.

As for members of the church and the week-to-week congregants and attendees, I did not check the tithing of those families on any systematic or regular basis. I did, however, on occasion—every year or so—review a similar list from the bookkeeper. Why, you might ask? Because, I believe a pastor should know how his or her people are doing spiritually, and I believe tithing and giving to be a spiritual matter. I believe that if I am called to disciple people, then it means in every aspect of biblical principles. I certainly wouldn't call individual families or question their financial giving, but the occasional awareness would primarily help me discern my own pastoral effectiveness in this arena.

I've never believed God's leaders should "sugar coat" things that Jesus spoke about, that the Bible teaches, or that we need in order to be faithful, accountable, honorable, and worshipful followers of Christ. Just give me truth. That's why I did it. Truth. For what it's worth, as said, I did not call members about what I might have seen or noticed in an annual, bi-annual, or random review of tithing reports. I only addressed this with church leaders. As pastor, I allowed the Lord to speak to me about how I was to lead and shepherd His people, about what I was to teach, and about how I was to disciple. I wanted to know, what is the spiritual condition of our people? They are God's people. It is God's Church. My ministry is not mine but God's, and He has entrusted it to me. It's all about Jesus, friends. It's all about Him.

I am called to disciple people.

Chapter 6

Standing in His Presence

L et's take a moment to discuss the dynamics of simply "standing in His presence" in a moment of quiet solitude and reverence. Waiting on the Lord is something that is too often foreign in today's Church. There are certain cultures that do this better than do others, but it should be something all churches and leaders are keenly aware of and cognizant of for their own "Day of Worship."

There were times during the pastorate that our Sunday mornings were surprisingly met with the unexpected (in a good way). While the Church's leaders should never be caught off guard by God's manifest presence, let's admit it, we all are amazed with His power and presence when it's so tangible that you feel as though you can touch it. There are many reading this who have no idea what this author is alluding too, but there are others who know exactly what I'm saying! For those who've never experienced the tangible, manifest presence of God, it is beyond amazing. It breaks down walls, delivers people from bondages, frees them of guilt and shame, fills them with joy unspeakable, and more. What does all that mean, and how does one attain it? While

I can't put a chart of 1-2-3 together to answer that question, I can tell you there are things a pastor should do and can do to welcome God's presence.

"I thought we brought the presence of the Lord with us when we come to church?" you might ask. Yes, that's true to an extent, for believers. They certainly have the living presence of God within, but I believe there is also scriptural reason to expect a corporate presence of God within the worship of God's people. It's in those times that we, as leaders, can move ahead with our agendas and schedules, formats and plans—or we can slow down just enough to purposefully wait for the presence of the Lord.

For those who've never experienced the tangible, manifest presence of God, it is beyond amazing.

One of the key elements to our church's mission and vision was to develop anointed praise and worship. Through the years, I was blessed to have gifted and anointed worshippers and musicians leading and new members from time to time joining our team. The music ministry at our church was excellent. It took time, effort, prayer, relationship building, and practice, but the friends who gave themselves to this area of ministry were a special group of leaders who humbly worked for the church's best interests. They offered each of us as worshippers the opportunity to meet God on a personal level.

In that type of environment there were moments during the pre-message praise and worship of the service when I could sense people in the audience yearning for more. There were times I saw tears flowing down the faces of people as they prayed or sang, or as they quietly stood there in their own moment of worship. Other times people would come to an altar and kneel in prayer during the music, at times before the message had even been offered. The blessing was in pressing in closer to the heart of God. This may feel uncomfortable for those who are new to His presence, but, just as giving birth is uncomfortable, still, the joy of life is overwhelming. When these intense moments occurred, it was not uncommon for me to walk to the podium and pause. I would simply stand in His presence. I would purposefully wait, saying nothing. I can remember to this day quietly praying, sometimes with tears in my own eyes, "Lord, please do Your work in the lives of our people today, and don't let me mess it up." I desperately wanted His presence and wanted people's lives and

I would purposefully wait, saying nothing.

hearts to find healing from the cares of life and the heartaches of the week past. God was faithful, and His manifest presence never ceased to amaze me when I welcomed it and waited for Him, and Him alone. I encourage pastors to be sensitive to those moments and if they have never done this previously, try it. Walk to the podium as the music lingers and simply stand in God's presence. You need not say a word. If given the opportunity,

God's presence will communicate clearly what needs to be heard in the hearts of every person present.

Chapter 7

Setting Social Media
Dos and Don'ts

In the original book in this series, *Setting the Atmosphere for the Day of Worship*, I briefly touched on social media, but there's far more to be said about the topic than even this added chapter can address. I've been told more than once that I post more than I should. And, have we all made some mistakes in the social media arena? Of course, we have. Let's address a few points that those in leadership should always remember, since this is a part of our world that isn't going away.

You can have a million great things to offer today's generations, old and young, but if your social media sends the wrong impressions or portrays a persona of someone people don't want to be around, then you've given off an "ugh" kind of vibe, and they won't want to hear from you on any of the other topics you think they want and need. If you tend to be frustrated constantly about a particular topic or audience group and it shows in your social media negativity, most anything else you would want to communicate that is meaningful and strengthening will be totally overlooked.

Why? The answer is quite simply that you are viewed as negative and most do not want to follow, read, or give their energy to negativity.

It was a summer day, mid-week, 90+ degrees on a sunny New Jersey beach when I asked three Gen Ys and Gen Xs (family and friends) their opinions of a few of these topics. Here are some of the things I learned from their

Indiscriminate frenzies aren't helpful to anyone's witness.

honest responses:

- Indiscriminate frenzies aren't helpful to anyone's witness. Be careful what and when you post.

- Don't be super-spiritual, and don't be weird. Just because something you've seen on YouTube is encouraging to you doesn't mean it offers the same meaning to others.

- Avoid messaging people you don't really know. There's etiquette to this journey. Use some cautions.

- Avoid mass messaging in general, but especially don't randomly post 50-100 tags of something you're selling or something you think is "the greatest gift to the world" or whatever. That's just not right.

- Don't act like it's a text when you're on your favorite social media venue; remember it's not private.

- Don't use social media as your platform to criticize or call people out. That should be done in person, privately, or not at all.

- As a pastor, keep your personal media personal. It's not the church's billboard.
- Do promote church events, but again, the church should be a separate account.
- If you do a social media messaging of anyone of the opposite sex, make it a group text or message, so as to provide accountability.
- Various accountability Apps, such as *Covenant Eyes*, can provide assistance.
- If an individual in the youth group messages a youth pastor the youth pastor should make a new thread to make it public, including any spouses, or others in the group.
- Spell-check the things you post.
- Don't make personal remarks to people/individuals when commenting on someone else's posts.
- Keep your angry political rants off other's Facebook pages.
- Always be encouraging.
- Physical compliments are a "no-no." "You all look so happy" works just as well.
- If you're viewing or searching months or years-past photos of various Facebook friends, don't comment on the photos. It's awkward and odd. Are you a stalker? They may think that of you.
- If you see a photo that someone has posted, don't force a spiritual moment, with "I'm praying for you...

or whatever." But, if you want to tell someone you're praying for them, then send them a personal message. It's far more appropriate.

Most certainly high levels of success can be achieved from correct usage of social media venues. Your effective presence on social media can bring you great productivity and return for your businesses, community, or professional platforms. Facebook is a great tool, especially for my generation, to keep up with families and friends and stay connected to one another's worlds, but the sad reality is that one never really knows if it is actually their "real" world or not, let alone the concerns of determining if it's a fake duplicated account from an imposter or the actual friend with whom you think you're communicating. Concerns about phishing and hackers have caused a number of leaders to shy away from "accepting" or "inviting" when using platforms of this nature. Then, there's the challenge of being disciplined enough oneself to avoid commenting on every post you see. That's a lesson we all need to learn. You don't have to comment. There's no need to make your voice known on every topic, especially if that topic rattles your cage.

You don't have to comment.

One extraordinary young leader told me related to what they feel about Facebook, that too often people post things that are difficult to receive. It makes users think to themselves when reading such articles posted by others, "I know you, and I really want to think well of you, but you post things that are so mean and derogatory about other people that I don't like it, and it makes me struggle to like you." How many preachers, pastors, church members, and so-called "Christians" of the community, fall into that category? Likely, too many fit that description.

Unfortunately, there is often too much freedom on social media. The message many pastors or church leaders think they are sending by their posts, which possibly they could get away with in a more personal or private setting, simply would not be acceptable in other public arenas. You know what I'm addressing. Those Facebook posts that are rants, or inadvertently calling someone out in church through a passive-aggressive post, are totally inappropriate. All church leaders should be held to the same level of accountability. Churches should be encouraging, and they should promote God, family, and the outreaches and missions of the church itself. Your social media platform is always on display and always sending a message. Be sure your message is

Your social media platform is always on display and always sending a message.

about the things that matter! It is easy to get caught up in the spotlight, especially if certain people are feeding into your ego, but you shouldn't allow that to stain your public witness or your private spiritual discernment. I am disheartened to think that some pastors seem to work more on being Internet-popular than spiritually effective.

Remember your calling and purpose. Simply stated, perhaps church leaders, especially, should recognize that their on-line presence is also a witness—whether good or bad.

People seem so entitled on social media. We're not entitled. That should be a key social media gauge. Social media can create false realities sometimes. People spend a lot of time to make their lives look happy and picture-perfect, but those images can be a false portrayal about life. It's acceptable to have issues, problems, or challenges. The Barbie doll mentality of life is false and unhealthy. It's challenging to be truthful and transparent on social media. But, do it. In so doing, ponder whether or not you actually want to post that photo or type that sentence.

Have complete social profiles. Be consistent. Be engaging. Brand yourself uniquely. Regularly interact with your networks. Be entertaining and informative. Use correct content for the specific media you're using at the time. Be visually appealing. Be generous and give credit to others where credit is due. Be positive, empower, and inspire.

On that topic, be inspiring, not needy. Use balance in your content and exercise caution not to over-share the same messages. We get it. Trust me. Use appropriate and proper grammar. As mentioned previously, spell things correctly. Avoid using all CAPS, which is considered SHOUTING online, and shy away from too many #hashtags. Be a lifter, not a downer. Be humble, and avoid coming off as a know-it-all. Be real and work to avoid sounding like you're the most spiritual person in the world implying everyone else is less-than. If you're down on your church, your fellowship, your denomination, your family, your whatever, just remember that social media is not the place to air that laundry or rant. Such a post is not as spiritual as you may think. It turns people off, including me.

Before you tweet, text, e-mail, tumble, vibe, WhatsApp, foursquare, Link, blog, flicker, vimeo, YouTube, Skype, snap chat, telegram, reddit, taringa, myface, snapfish, meetme, meetup, vero, or any of the other alternative social media platforms, consider the basics before you type and send. Not everything you read on-line is true. Double check veracity. Are you helping anyone by offering your opinions? The words you've clicked may be what are in your head at the moment, but do they inspire? Have you just offended someone by what you posted? Is it even necessary for you to say what you're about to say? Just use common sense, God-given wisdom, and reflect on what you're saying and doing before you hit send.

Celebrating the Voice of Your Spouse: Having Renee on the Platform

I f you're not married, read this chapter anyway. One never knows whether it may be beneficial in the future.

The amazing leader and professional in her own right that she is, Renee was never one to be up front too often in our ministry. When we pastored a local church, she led and was involved in various ministries, as nearly every pastor's spouse does. She was faithful to our bus ministry for years, taught a Sunday school class for kids, worked with the church women, found opportunities for hospitality, and more. However, she would rarely appear before the people by standing on the platform. She left that to me. She didn't sing on the worship team, play keyboard or piano as a church musician (though she does play piano beautifully, and made sure both our children learned to play, as well), or minister very often from behind the pulpit.

I learned early on, though—and I think this is a lesson

pastors today need to discover all the sooner—on the rare occasions I would have Renee stand beside me in the pulpit, or be with me publicly in view of the congregation, the deeper, clearer, and stronger would be our integrity and reliability as a team. She was and is my best friend. Her ministry beside mine is and was crucial through anything we would navigate. After all we are married and she and I are a team.

We've all heard it said somewhere, sometime, for pastors, one's spouse could make or break him or her. In my case, my dear wife won me points every time she would come to my side. If you are married, I pray that you, as a leader, will find those moments where God's people can find strength, hope, and confidence in the godly couple at the helm of their ministries.

If you are married, and your spouse is struggling, this can sometimes unfortunately be a hindrance to the work of pastoring God's church. Let me encourage you to love your spouse with all your heart, find trusted counselor(s) who can walk with you both through the journeys of leadership, and use discernment and wisdom as to how and when you position your spouse in a role he or she may or may not be comfortable with—and one, to which your people also may or may not be comfortable.

Renee's voice was important during those years of our pastoring a congregation. As we led in ministry together I learned early in the journey that she had a keen sense of ... you need to be cautious ... Or, I sense.... Or, I feel I should warn you to be careful around "so and so." That's what this chapter is addressing, and more. If you are married, your spouse is your "help meet" as the Bible says Eve was fitting for Adam. Take that to heart. You're in this together for a purpose. Let the Lord develop and use that in you both over the years for the betterment of the church.

Whether you're a hugger or a more cautious and private distanced-leader (there's not a right or a wrong), I encourage leaders of God's church to simply (1) know their audience, (2) work within the context and framework of the ministry in which they are placed, (3) be true to their own personality and "mojo," (4) carefully, respectfully, and honorably know the ground rules for what's acceptable or not in any given context, and (5) trust their spouse's judgment (if you've been given the gift of a spouse) to help you know the first four points above.

> *You're in this together for a purpose.*

I tell you these things because they're important. When Renee and I were youth pastors, she came to me once and said, "You need to be cautious around _____." I was simultaneously serving as the church's worship leader at the time and was before the people weekly. I said, "Renee, you're crazy. She's old enough to be my mother." You know what? Just a few years later, that woman divorced her husband... and ... well, let's just say, Renee had a keen sense of protecting her "clueless and trusting" young husband.

Just a few years later when I was an associate pastor, Renee came to me once and said, "Something's off. Something's not right in that situation." I said, "Renee, you're crazy. That's nonsense. Surely, not." Guess what? Within a year, two families we loved and trusted were getting divorces, and Renee's inclinations were proving true. Though I didn't listen in these two instances, time and time again since then, I've been able to trust the balance and spiritual discernment of my dear wife as she reminds me to not hug the teenager, to be sure to give a side-hug to the women in church, to consciously shake the hand of the husband first, or be spiritually and keenly aware of what's right or not for the moment. These things are key for today's spiritual leaders. It's called integrity. Heeding Renee's advice brought balance to me as well as stability and strength to our entire church family.

Chapter 9

Acknowledging the Value of Affiliation

I have a number of friends who are Independent, Non-denominational, Catholic, Methodist, Presbyterian, Lutheran, Nazarene, Southern Baptist, Missionary Baptist, Freewill Baptist, Anglican, Episcopal, Assemblies of God, Church of God, Charismatic, from North American Christian denominations, and more. Quite simply put, I love God's Church. It is remarkable on many levels. It's not perfect. People structure it, but it's a striking creation of God's covenant and character in and among His people.

Years ago, I penned a foundational basis for why I felt it was meaningful for me to be a part of the ecclesiastical affiliation which I am privileged to serve. Through the years that document has seen revisions of various kinds. I've read similar writings from colleagues and have had multiple discussions over the years as to my thoughts.

Allow me, then, to offer from my lens the values of the Fellowship I serve. If you are a part of another ecclesiastical body, you may want to read this chapter in light of how your group functions. Possibly you will want to examine the values you find in your affiliation(s), as well. If you are independent or non-denominational, no doubt you too have strong convictions about where you are and why you're there. That's beautiful, as long as your group's convictions are scriptural

It's important to know where you stand, why you stand there, and how it impacts you, your family, and others.

and healthy. After all, even being independent or non-denominational is its own classification. It's important to know where you stand, why you stand there, and how it impacts you, your family, and others for their faith in Christ for years to come. All of us, regardless of affiliation, are accountable to one another, to the church, to our spouses if we are married, and to our families. However, there is one name, one man, one Savior, Redeemer, Deliverer, and Healer who matters most and to whom we are accountable—Jesus.

Throughout Church history, denominational lines have become distorted; certainly the evangelical world specifically has seen trends toward abandoning denominations altogether. I have heard it said that leaving denominations gives the local church freedom. Really? In my opinion accountability for leadership and the protections offered to God's people provide far more spiritual, doctrinal, and emotional support than do the intermittent and occasionally perceived as hierarchical interventions of a denominational office. When I came to Christ, I purposefully placed myself under authority; His and those to whom He would place over me. I welcome and desire Godly influencers to speak into my life and guide the intentions of my heart. The Church is better served when God's leaders receive respectfully one from another. Have you ever met someone who seems to have no respect for authority or concept of being under authority? Certainly you have, as have I, and it's not usually a pretty picture.

I'll never forget one church service I was obligated to attend within weeks of becoming a state denominational leader. The church leaders had convinced a local congregation that they should simply vote themselves out of the denominational affiliation and take the property and ministries for themselves independently. The church had been a ministry in the fellowship for decades, and the assets and ministries had been built and directed through the years with faithful members of the movement. The pastor leading the charge had inherited the ministry, building, and assets and now somehow felt that he should just be able to take it for himself, owning it for the new ministry he was forging independently. I'd like to say this was an isolated incident, but though they are rare, in my many years of leadership, this scenario has crossed my desk more than once. In this particular case, though, a member of the pastor's family stood up and in so many words proudly proclaimed to the audience—in my presence, I might add—that it was their opinion the church was in bondage and would finally be free if they no longer had to be accountable to the organization.

Malcolm Burleigh, the Executive Director of U.S. Missions for the Assemblies of God, is often overheard saying, "You can't be in authority if you're not under it." They did not want to be accountable.

What exactly does a church do when leaders structure the church in a way that there's little to no accountability? That's a good question. How does the membership respond when all or many of the board members are family members or simply appointed affirmative voters? Surely no one would embezzle or misappropriate funds from the tithes and offerings. After all, we've all known for years the one person who solely counts the money, deposits the money, writes all the checks, signs all the checks, and makes all the deposits and payments. By now, you might foresee that was a sarcastic statement that no one would ever misappropriate funds. Unfortunately, however, I have seen more than once when I or a colleague would need to step in to offer assistance to congregations after thousands of dollars have finally been noticed as missing, and church mortgage payments have somehow gone unpaid for months, only to find that the payments everyone *thought* were being made to the church's bank account were being made to someone *else's* favor. That reality poses a dilemma on multiple elements when such behavior is finally noticed.

Additionally, how does a church handle erroneous scriptural or theological teachings and ministry if no one is available to offer training to the pastor(s) and there is nowhere to go for any ecclesiastical accountability? The easy answer of telling those churches to look to their Constitution and Bylaws may be well meaning but is too often shallow, because they likely do not have documents that define well their needs at that moment (though they should have). Worse yet, if they have a document of sorts, they may not have seen it in years nor do they even know where to look to find it. You get the picture. Such scenarios can quickly become dicey, uncomfortable, conflict-ridden, and even litigious.

I am affiliated with the Assemblies of God. What are reasons I love being a minister in this global movement? Here are just a few:

Doctrine

I believe in what this Fellowship preaches. Our Fellowship's doctrine is 66 books and from that our AG forebears saw fit to lay down 16 Fundamental Truths that we deem non-negotiable. I can tell my children who are global travelers that if they attend an Assemblies of God church affiliate anywhere in the world, the basic premise of the church will be just like they found at home. Styles may change. The message is (for the most part) a unified constant. The protectorate of doctrinal purity provides a path of light and hope for today's Church in a world of watered-down messages and politically correct opinions promoted by the masses.

Missions and Global Impact

I believe in doing what Jesus said (see Matt 28:19-20), and my church believes in missions. In *Redemptive Missiology in Pneumatic Context*, I offer details of the missionary endeavors for our Fellowship. That said, the commitment of the AG (now almost 1 percent of the global population based on 2018 AG Statistics acknowledging 69+ million adherents in more than 370,000 churches) from the beginning until now—to be a missionary church with indigenous principles led by the Holy Spirit until all have heard—remains the core of this great church. I love it!

Accountability

Knowing I have Bible-solid leaders who will aid me in remaining biblically and theologically sound in my ministry brings peace of mind. If disciplinary action were needed (and unfortunately it happens), there are wise counselors who keep redemption and healing as their objectives in helping ministers and/or congregations work through the pains of brokenness.

Training and Leadership Resources

If my heart and goal is to produce Spirit-empowered disciples, then the strategic parameters of my own efforts for continued education, training, discipleship, and mobilization are paramount to the fruit I bear. From our organization's amazing events and ministries for every demographic in the church—(nursery to seniors), to summer camps for kids and teens, to emergency assistance when times get tough, to every help imaginable for those desiring ministry credentialing—I could not imagine taking this journey without my Fellowship.

Pastoral Transitions and Assistance for Churches to Find New Pastors

Early in my ministry as a denominational superintendent, I found myself receiving phone calls from leaders of independent churches in need of lead pastors. They would offer their hopes that I would consider sending them one of our Fellowship's dozens to hundreds of names of credentialed and trained ministers as potential candidates for their independent churches. There is likely no more significant moment in the life of a church than the season of finding God's leader for the pastorate. The challenges are many for congregations without trained and anointed leadership. Those independent churches who would call me in those early days had apparently learned what I had witnessed already. The resources found from screened, interviewed, seasoned, background-checked, and proven ministry individuals were discovered readily in nearby denominational offices.

Women in Ministry

While there are still a good number of churches that challenge this theological interpretation, I stand wholeheartedly defending the scriptural ministry of Miriam, a prophet to Israel during the Exodus (Exod 15:20); another woman prophet, Huldah (2 Kgs 22:14-20; 2 Chron 34:22-28); the New Testament's Tabitha (Dorcas) who ran benevolence ministries (Acts 9:36); and myriad other female ministers and church leaders from Euodia and

Syntyche, Clement, Priscilla, Mary, Phoebe, Junia, Deborah, and more. *See: Footnote[1]

Fellowship

Few can understand how lonely one can feel while serving in ministry. For ministers and church leaders often seen as public role models always ready to address the crowd, take the photo, or lead the way, it can be one of the loneliest career paths on earth. Finding confidants and faithful friends who can handle hearing the truth of a minister's challenges and heartaches is rare indeed. Being together in the journey with those of like precious faith for personal and interpersonal reassurances and inspiration is essential for ministry health.

I'm grateful to "belong," to be a part of the Fellowship that offers me accountability and spiritual covering. Hopefully you, too, can say the same about yours.

---

[1] "The Role of Women in Ministry." Assemblies of God (USA) Official Web Site. https://ag.org/Beliefs/Position-Papers/The-Role-of-Women-in-Ministry (accessed January 14, 2020).

$$Chapter\ 10$$

Painting the Children's Church Walls

"Do you want the *adults* to like it, or do you want the *kids* to like it?" That's exactly what Patsy Dennis said to me when I questioned the proposed multi-colors, graffiti paintings, and (what I considered, initially) busy and trying characters for the children's wing walls. Our extraordinary children's pastor, who would some years later be the denominational state children's ministries director, had hired a graffiti artist from a nearby city to paint each room and wall of the children's wing. I assumed a "genuine" artist was going to paint. He did, but with spray paint cans. It was quite a sight to see. Gratefully, he was indisputably a graffiti specialist, and his accompanying tattoos somehow did aid me in feeling more comfortable that he apparently knew what he was doing. When it was all complete, the kids loved it, and the art drew them back happily week-to-week when they would experience a significant worship service our remarkable children's church team had designed. It was fun, interactive, age-appropriate, time-sensitive, and exciting, and filled with heart-impacting worship, prayer, and lessons. This was no babysitting service. These kids had a worship service that served them long into their adult lives and was a standard-bearer for what many would someday look for in a children's church environment for their own children.

During these years, I learned a few lessons. First, there are a number of ways to build a house. Years later, I used that analogy numerous times. Of course, there's a certain way I like it built, but when you trust your leaders, you give them the tools to lead. Don't micro-manage. Is it possible the house will be built differently than if you physically built it yourself? Yes, it is. Is it possible you could do it better? Well, that's based on one's perception, but yes, it's possible. Nonetheless, if I can't trust my team, then why are they in leadership *on* my team? Why would I keep them on my staff or church leadership if I can't have full confidence in them and rely on them to appropriately handle the matters I'm leaning on them to accomplish?

> *This was no babysitting service.*

Trust your leaders to make you better—with their gifts, perceptions, and talents (in their own specific and unique areas)—than you are yourself. That's what leaders do; they make us better with their presence on the team than we could ever be on our own. Trust your leaders even when it comes to chairing your meetings, conferences, and seminars. While certainly there are meetings that only the leader should lead, if you can't trust your key team to run a meeting in your absence, then you have a bigger problem than you think. Choose leaders faithful in their spiritual walk, loyal in their dedication, competent in their fields, teachable, humble, accountable, and trusted by others.

Often, Dad picks the house, Mom picks the cars, and the kids pick the church. Or, maybe for you it was Mom picking the house and Dad choosing your vehicles, but you get the point. Almost always, it is the children who ultimately pick the family's church. You can fight that all you want, but the last part is true regardless. I have walked into several churches throughout my years, and no matter how amazing the speaking and worship was, if the kid's didn't like it, it was over before it was given a chance! Your kid's ministry matters! Allow me to rephrase it, it's a "DEAL BREAKER or GAME CHANGER" on whether families stay or continue their church shopping. Kids ministry is not a weekend functional day-care. It's a ministry with interaction, worship, teaching time, giving challenges, and games, and yes, it needs to be fun!

Maybe you're saying, "It's not all about games and fun!" Well, if it's not fun, then start practicing your good-byes instead of hellos. Maybe you don't have the right teacher, rooms, or greeters, but you *do* have a can of paint and can buy some incredible lights; you can be on time, be groomed, and wear the same kids ministry T-shirt. There are plenty of things one can do to dig into the beginning phase of retaining and growing young families at your church. If you want to minister to them spiritually, you have to attract them naturally with things that will draw their attention to give you an honest chance.

There's a world of *wow* when exciting attention gets drawn to any specific area of your church. Attract new families, and watch kids' eyes light up when they walk in the door. It makes a huge difference to parents also, when their kids are counting the hours on Saturday night to get to go to their church the next day or better yet, counting the days from midweek on until they get to come back to church. It can be reality. I've lived it. And it can be reality in your

The children's ministry is too important to be casual and unengaging.

church, also. Fresh and creative ideas bring sensory imagination and amazing expression to young hearts exploring new worlds. Use vibrant colors and make it welcoming. The children's ministry is too important to be casual and unengaging. Again, our kids LOVED the walls. The crowds of kids, their joy, laughter, and excitement week to week about returning, all these things soon proved their value to me and to parents. I was glad when I went to the house of the Lord and the children's pastor had painted the walls of the children's church rather than trusting me for the task.

Chapter 11

Hiring and Firing

I 'll begin this chapter where I ended the last. In my opinion one should choose leaders who are faithful in their spiritual walk, loyal in their dedications, competent in their fields, teachable, humble, accountable, and trusted by others. The hiring of staff customarily is a momentous occasion. Often eagerness and anticipation fill the air.

Occasionally, though, a manager or leader has to fire employees as well. This firing of employees is unfortunate and delicate, but critical to the health or life of an organization. In over thirty years of ministry, I've only needed to release a handful of staff. I can honestly say that each time, I actually waited as graciously and as long as I could—far longer than any other leader I know—before making the decision to "pull the trigger." While situations may have varied by the time that I had endured enough angst, I obviously had been brought to a point where I determined it was the last straw when I made the decision needed. Even with the most difficult of situations, where I found myself having to deal with really good people yet realizing the health of the ministry could no longer tolerate the missteps or dealings with them that brought disunity and despair, by this stage of the game the verdicts at that point were not arduous. The moments of "the meeting" or the time of communicating the decision and plan, to this day, still create prickly feelings and troubling memories. No doubt those meetings can be awkward or uneasy if you are prone to your own emotional issues of feeling badly about having to let someone go. Though it may sound difficult, it's easier if you are simply respectful but direct. Remember, the organization as a whole depends on your leadership to lead the team with integrity, vision, and health.

The hope of a brighter tomorrow wins out every time, and when you've prayed and are confident it's the right thing for the organization, you can rest assured it's also the correct thing for the individual. The Bible promises that God directs the steps of righteous people. We simply have to trust that truth and to be respectful, confident, and courageous in leadership. It's what leaders do.

> *Remember, the organization as a whole depends on your leadership to lead the team with integrity, vision, and health.*

Let me also suggest that you create and use (to some extent) defined job descriptions. Having such descriptions is more challenging for small churches or small office environments, but it is still a key principle to follow when those uncertain or unexpected moments arrive when you need to cut someone loose or process a transition you hadn't expected.

Senior personnel may set the pace or agendas for your office, ministry, or timely initiatives. However, in smaller businesses or churches it is often administrative team members who understand far more detail about day-to-day operations, jobs to be completed, or specific tasks that bring the rhythm required for synthesis and efficiency. When you trust your team implicitly, there is nothing wrong with letting them help you design the structures needed for new hires, the details of job descriptions, and the insights needed for success down the road. Your new hires will impact all of their daily routines. Let your key administrative team members help senior leaders be as successful as possible for the team's overall performance in decisions, training, and assessments. I've been blessed with amazingly gifted and competent team members on my staff through the years that have always made me better than I am by myself. I wish the same for you!

Don't shy away from positive encouragement for your staff. Likewise, don't avoid evaluating conversations, discipline, and precautionary deliberations, both verbal and written—all as needed. Through the years there have been times I used actual written evaluations, and then there were other periods when I chose not to do annual reviews. Do what works best in your environment. Don't just do something because the big church down the street does it or the business-owning members of the church say that's

> *Don't shy away from positive encouragement for your staff.*

how they do it in their company that appears to be prospering. Do what's right for you, your church environment, and your leaders. Just remember, whatever you do, be fair and deliberate in your decisions as you help an employee transition. If you need a written document signed by all parties, then do so. Keep things clean, above board, and done with clarity for all to understand.

Later in this book when I address conflict management, I speak about a key to remember if you decide to resign. You'll want to read that section. Also, if you're the lead pastor, manager, or project guide, and a team member offers you a resignation, you'll find in that section a truth you don't want to miss.

When unity has been lost, trust displaced, loyalty disregarded, standards abandoned, competence vanished, or the innumerable other considerations that will sometimes drive you to that place of terminating someone's employment or service, do so only after you've found peace in committed prayer, further direction from trusted colleagues who have offered counsel and reason, and total confidence from the Lord that you're standing on solid ground. Those guides will give you the strength needed to make the right decisions at the right time for your organization, church, or ministries.

Chapter 12

Making Nominations, Elections, and Appointments

Let's begin this discussion by considering those moments when a leader needs to appoint someone for a title, position, or strategic role. Just as with hiring a new team member, do so only after you have considered the varying factors that can give you and others confidence in the appointment after it's been made. Have you seen the individual in action? Do you know their background, successes, and failures? Are their personalities such that would be a good fit for your present team? Do they bring things to the table that are critical, strategically sought after, and helpful to the progression of your organization's vision, goals, and dreams? Are they loyal, teachable, accommodating, and likely most importantly, competent? Of course, don't forget that what we do is spiritual. Are they spiritual people? Do they have a deep and trusted faith walk? If they do, most other things will work out, provided they are competent. Did I remind you that it's important they be ... *competent*?

It helps to have references. It simply amazes me how many companies, chief leaders, or managers do not take the extra effort to contact references. If you receive references, take the time to contact them and find out what they might have to say about your potential appointees. Certainly, most references will give positive feedback (that's why we as individuals use them as references). However, you'll be amazed what details you can learn about a person, and what honesty some references will offer, even if you're not specifically asking for it. It is remarkable what particulars you may not have known or thought of regarding the candidate if you'll just make the calls and contact the references listed.

During the years of my pastorate, I would have an annual business meeting for the purpose of electing church officers, board members, etc. In the earlier years, I was at the mercy of a hopeful heart when that annual meeting arrived trusting that nominations and elections would go smoothly and that no one individual or their families would be in any way offended, even if inadvertently. Then, a few years into the journey I decided to not work harder, but smarter. I sat down with key leadership, board members, and a few instrumental staff to devise a board member nomination process that would best fit our needs. That time and effort saved our ministries and me a world of headaches in the years to come. You should do what works best for you and your particular church. Not everything can simply be cookie-cutter, but, this is how ours turned out, and it was a stellar addition to our systems and procedures.

About a month before the annual business meeting I would prepare a cover letter explaining that we would be meeting for our annual meeting soon on such and such a date and that as members they were not only entitled to attend but should enjoy the opportunity of nominating other members to leadership roles to be filled at the meeting. I would enclose an active church membership list so recipients of the letter would have the names of all other members of the church readily available in their hands. The letter offered some of the basics regarding the positions to be filled by election and encouraged nominations only after a time of prayer, and a sense of genuine trust in the maturity of the leaders one may nominate. Also enclosed was a nomination form, which requested the name(s) of those they might nominate, as well as their own signature at the bottom of the form. Only signed forms were accepted. This provided accountability, as only actual members of the church could fill out and turn in a nomination form. The system worked well. The letter would offer a deadline to have the forms returned.

When all the nominations were received, names were tabulated, and I as pastor would receive a report listing each election nominee. As a part of the process, I created a nomination committee that would handle the initial screening of the names, contacting each nominee at a strategic moment in the process, etc. Doing that allowed me to comfortably remain everyone's pastor and avoid awkward moments that no one needed or wanted at that moment. The nomination committee handled the important task of ensuring key information. I didn't need to contact people in this scenario and ask the occasionally awkward question(s). Committee members would assume that role.

Was the nominee a member of the church? Were they qualified to serve? Were they faithful members in good standing? Now, that can be dicey! Were they individuals who would be helpful and prayerfully support the church and pastor's vision and dreams? We didn't just want "yes" people, but those supportive and encouraging to the ministry overall while inquisitive enough to bring great ideas to the table. Were there awkward matters (baggage) that might cause issues for the church, the pastor, the nominee, or their families if they were to be considered for an election at that time? The nomination committee would discuss all these matters and actually held the right to consider removal of names if they felt it in the best interests of the pastor or the church. If it were suggested a name(s) be removed, that would be discussed with the pastor for further detail and clarifications before the committee would make decisions of that nature.

Further, each nominee received a letter in the mail with a nomination questionnaire asking them to personally offer much of the information needed prior to those calls or contacts. Beginning with an encouraging word that they should feel honored to have gained such respect from other members to have their name nominated, the letter also requested their answers to many questions posed that would help us know those who "might be" laboring among us, as the Bible says. The letter offered the nominee the respect of declining the nomination (by way of signature) and thus not needing to fill out the questionnaire. Or, if they opted to accept the nomination, they would then go on to fill out the questions listed. It was a simple system that worked well for us.

After those questionnaires were received, a committee member would then contact all nominees who had chosen to keep their name listed in the nomination. The pertinent questions would then be asked. Was the nominee willing to allow their name to be presented publicly to the church in consideration of the election? Did they feel it was a good season or a good time for them to serve? Could they commit to the needed meetings? Would their spouses and/or families be supportive if they took on the extra volunteer role for the church? Sometimes people have personal or mitigating circumstances that hinder their desire to serve at that time, or which cause them to hesitate in allowing their names to be presented for the election. If there are matters of that nature present, those are personal and not to be discussed publicly or questioned if a nominee offers to decline the nomination. I find that nominees are appreciative of being asked prior to the meeting, rather than simply showing up to a meeting and finding out (whether they wanted to serve or not) that their name has been presented publicly. It's much better to learn

It's much better to learn of things prior to an election than during one.

of things prior to an election than during one. Again, trust me.

After each of these decisions were confirmed, the nomination committee (about four key individuals—including two current and present board members, one staff person, and one lay leader or member of the church) would then prepare the updated short list of nominees and present it to the pastor. If there was any information learned that might cause a question or be pertinent for the pastor to personally follow up on, I would then begin making my contacts accordingly. Usually those were wonderful conversations and encouraging to the members who had received such confidence from other church members by way of this nomination. Occasionally for some, it was an opportunity for me, as pastor, to encourage members of our church who might be going through some trying times in their lives, their homes, or with their families at that moment. Pastoring people is one of the highest privileges in the world.

By the time election night came around, all leaders felt much better about the potential of what might occur, simply because a little time and effort had been put into the process in advance.

Chapter 13

Speaking in Other Churches

One of the surest ways to set an atmosphere that turns off the ears and hearts of searching souls is to be or be perceived as offensive to the people of God or those to whom you've been given the privilege to minister. Biblical literacy and truth is not offensive. I've seen individual speakers say and do things that simply should not have been said or done in front of particular audiences.

During the years I was pastoring, on certain occasions I would be honored with an invitation to preach in other churches in the community. On those occasions, I made it a point to respect other pastors' pulpits, varying denominational theologies, or anything that might cause concern or challenges to the pastor of that particular church. It is imperative to protect God's people from confusion. I believe if one is called to pastor in a local community he or she is called to pastor not just that particular church, but also the community at large. To be faithful to the post, one should never cause division or confusion. Rather, work to build bridges, unity, trust, and faith.

When invited to preach in a church of a different denomination than yours, or a church that might hold alternative theologies to you, keep in mind that the opportunity you've been given is rarely—if at all—the time to convince people that your doctrine is correct, and theirs needs to be tweaked. Just don't do that. It's not right. I've seen people do this, and I simply don't like it. The beautiful people of God don't deserve being led into confusion by someone proclaiming to have all truth or the only way to scriptural interpretation. An invited guest should always respect the people of God and the pastor of the house. If you

Work to build bridges, unity, trust, and faith. feel you shouldn't preach there, then don't. It's that simple. Further, respect for the Lord matters even more. There are sixty-six books of the Bible and plenty that can be preached to bless the church and lead a wanderer to the foot of the Cross without worrying about doctrinal differences at that instant.

Few things can help build community relationships with neighboring churches and ministries better than getting to know the city's pastors well enough to comfortably invite one or two to join your church in ministry on occasion. Have you ever considered finding a few circumstances where you could invite neighboring pastors, even those of other denominations, to preach at your church? While it might not be a consideration you'd want to do regularly (every situation is different), it can make for strategic relationship building, and you might just make a friend! If you do this, do it thoughtfully, and make sure you authentically know and can vouch for the minister you're giving your pulpit to for the service. We as pastors are responsible for our leadership of God's people and God's church. Make sure the atmosphere you set, the atmosphere you allow, or endorse, brings glory and honor to the Lord and allows God's people the best chance of hearing His Word and meeting His presence.

Chapter 14

Look Up. Look Down.
Look Across.

What ever happened to humility and teamwork? What happened to unpretentiousness and cooperation? Collaboration and solidarity is what the Church should embody, so I am a strong proponent of church leaders, churches within the community, and certainly individual fellowships working together and encouraging one another in the work of the harvest. We're all in this together. Rivalry has crept into the church, and it's heartbreaking. Churches competing with one another, pastors feeling they have to compare with the church down the street for outreaches, events, big days, attendance records, facilities, and more are all unfortunately a part of today's Church mainstream. Small churches and rural or new church plants struggling with "keeping up with the Joneses" is a disheartening reality. No wonder non-believers (those most often good people, who quite simply with integrity admit they are not sold on the God of the Bible or a personal relationship thing with Jesus) often wonder about what the church has to offer. If I see competition among churches and her leaders, I'm willing to suggest that those good people do, too.

Clarence St. John, an apostolic, church-planting, former Superintendent of the Minnesota Assemblies of God, first shared this Up-Down-Across concept with me a number of years ago, giving me consent to use it as it might best fit into our Kentucky fellowship's context. I believed it, and still do. I used it and urged others to do the same.

The small church leader(s) should be **looking up** and finding churches and leaders who can help them in the journey. The church of twenty-five should be building relationships with the church fifty. The church of fifty should be building relationships with the church of 100. The church of 500 should be building relationships with the church of 1,000, and so on. They should be looking up. There's much to gain by having a friend who's been there before and already worked through some of the leadership and structural matters that could help me be more effective at what I'm called to do.

It goes both ways, of course. Also, we should **look down**. If you pastor one of your area's stronger churches, or if there's a church nearby (whether your denomination or not) that could use your help, or use your perfectly good discipleship or teaching materials you are no longer using, then why not offer it to them and help them out? Churches of 1,000 or 500 should look for the church of 250, 100, fifty, or even fewer, offering much-needed encouragement and assistance for their Kingdom work.

Look Up. Look Down. Look Across.

Too often church leaders of 350, 500, or 1000 or more are inappropriately perceived to be exclusive, less participative, or less welcoming to those who pastor "the Church of America—the small church." I've found the opposite to be usually true. They're frequently not exclusive or less participatory out of a weakened character trait. They're simply busy. Growing a church is hard work, and as the church grows, the staff will grow, budgets grow, and so do calendar challenges. All of this impacts what they can or cannot attend or do. While this doesn't relieve pastors and leaders of those churches from being team-players and participating for the larger cause, they do deserve the benefit of the doubt before the smaller churches or other leaders judge them mistakenly for what can be

Let's get to know and build relationships with neighboring leaders.

perceived as a slight at times. What one perceives as reality, though, does not lessen the mantle that church leaders wear to responsibly work together in the fields of harvest. We need one another, and if there's a church near me, or a pastor, leader, or staff person near me that I can assist, why wouldn't I want to offer them a helping hand, to aid them in being as effective as possible for the Kingdom? Am I really all that concerned if I pastor a church of 200, that the church of fifty, or a 100, is going to steal my church's people, or that somehow my helping them will endanger the ministry the Lord has entrusted to me? Let's "look down" (you get the point) to a church smaller than ours and take the pastor for lunch, coffee, or breakfast. Let's get to know and build relationships with neighboring leaders.

And, this next thought could be a stretch for some, but that's why I share it. I'm convinced it's time that the Church work together to reach those in the community that are yet to meet Christ and His amazing grace! Yes, I (some may say, naively) still believe we can work together in unity to do something remarkable for the Lord! Can Baptists and Methodists work together on occasion? Of course they can. Can Pentecostals and Lutherans or Presbyterians, Baptists, Methodists, or Catholics, all find a way on occasion to bless their overall communities? Yes, they can! Don't judge one another. Find what you can in common and do something together for Jesus. In other words, we can all **look across** the aisle to our neighboring churches—down the street, across town, across the street, or wherever, to offer our linked arms for ministries that could bring hope and life to the communities we're called to serve. It's okay to share your toys, play well together, work well with others. And, it just might be fun!

Chapter 15

Understanding Key Elements to a Healthy Church

Through the years these eight simple elements to a healthy church became my focus for preaching and ministry effectiveness:

- Praise and Worship
- Anointed Preaching of the Word
- Missions
- Soul Winning
- Prayer
- Discipleship
- Serving
- Reproducing/Planting

Praise and Worship

Often music is a challenge, especially for smaller or rural churches. Still, there are varying and productive ways that your song service, your "praise and worship" (as it is often called), and your atmosphere for the day of worship can be anointed and meaningful to all who attend. If you have one person who can offer musicianship, I suggest that you go "unplugged" (simply the one guitar or keyboard). If you need to use "canned worship" (i-worship or other similar tools), those work great, too! If you don't have God-gifted singers who are worshippers, then don't force that point. Use one person, unplugged (as mentioned), opting to hold several months of worship team practice on off nights, as needed, to develop the team you hope for and desire to use in the days ahead. Implement only when you feel you're as ready as possible.

I've also found that too many pastors, especially those new to the church, often think it's imperative that they change the styles of songs their congregants have been accustomed to for the last numbers of years. While that can be an important goal to attain (every situation is different), my advice is to not be too concerned about styles, graces, elegances, or what one might consider polishes—whether contemporary, traditional, hymns, full band, orchestra, *a cappella*, country, even bluegrass (I'm from Kentucky), a blend, or whatever. What matters is whether or not your people are passionate about what they're singing.

Focus on the heart. God has a way of taking care of the rest.

Anointing is present when worship is taking place. If they're only singing a song, the style won't matter, and the singing won't be any more drawing for "setting the atmosphere" regardless of what song list or style you choose to incorporate. Focus on the heart. God has a way of taking care of the rest.

Anointed Preaching of the Word

This is significant for setting the atmosphere so that guests and attendees will find meaningful and life-changing worship experiences when they come to your church. Improving your messages can be done in a number of ways. I suggest you read the Bible more, and I suggest you pray more. Be biblically literate and Holy Spirit discerning. There are a number of other tools that can assist your efficiency and effectiveness. Look at the length of your messages. The services are not more anointed simply because they're longer. Understand your context and your audience. Remember, usually our goal is to encourage them to return, not give them reasons not to. Learn to use vocal cues—highs, lows, inflections—that affirm or impact, facial expressions, eye contact, and various gestures. Those are basic communication skills that every professional orator learns to develop.

There's nothing like knowing your text well. I'm not saying you need to memorize it, but having the Word in your heart makes all the difference. It is a lamp and a light highlighting the path for all who hear. The Word does not return void. It always makes its point, so know the Word.

Another suggestion for preaching is to not wax too long on personal family stories. Be careful how much you use your family and children in illustrations. Why not have someone measure this for you by listening with a helpful but critical ear, marking with pen and paper, every time you use a certain illustration about your family or a particular re-occurring thematic point? This will help you learn your idiosyncrasies and address them for maximum impact when you walk to the pulpit.

As you minister, be organized in your points, and reiterate your main themes as needed while preaching or teaching. Though we like to think every parishioner listens attentively and remembers succinctly each point of every sermon we preach (because it's quite simply that good) that is not the case. Most will remember only a general sense of what your entire message is about, so reiterate your points and make it easy for listeners to have a few takeaways from the day. I know one pastor who recently moved his sermon styles to one-point messages, and it's working great! Do what works for you, but I wouldn't consider the ten-point or the fifteen-point sermons if you want people to remember or return. Again, trust me. I've done that a few times, and it's not good. I'm grateful my parishioners didn't throw things at me!

Of course, using visual graphics such as Keynote, Visme, PowerPoint, or one of a series of other similar tools will help make your points impactful and memorable. Be passionate about what you preach. That's key. Use a systems guide to make sure you preach on certain topics periodically throughout the year (helping avoid simply preaching the same things you always lean toward—grace, etc.). I found in the years of preaching ministry that the more you preach, the more comfortable and focused you become in the art of preaching. If you've never read a book on homiletics, do so, and, don't be afraid to ask your spouse, key leaders, or friends to offer you critiques. It will helps you get better. If you have availability to watch a video of you preaching your message, doing so will give you a first-hand view of your style, or lack of it. The key is to do all you can to prepare, practice, and pray so others might find His presence. Remember, He can do more in the blink of an eye than all the Sundays of preaching on your annual calendar, so make sure your worship moments count. People's lives and eternities are depending on it.

Missions

A missions-focused church will be blessed and growing. Mission-directed leaders and pastors will see more salvations, water baptisms, Spirit baptisms, and local and global impact for the Kingdom. If you haven't read *Redemptive Missiology in Pneumatic Context*, then do so. I offered an entire book focused on the Holy Spirit's work in a missions-minded church. This is likely one of the most important points of this chapter. I encourage you to not take missions lightly. I've heard too many pastors tell me through the years how they "definitely give energy to missions," then I find out their idea of giving it significance is quite different than mine would be, and in my opinion than that of Jesus, himself.

> *A missions-focused church will be blessed and growing.*

Soul-winning

Soul-winning is listed as its own category. "Isn't that the same as missions?" one might ask. Well, not exactly. While mission work is potentially soul-winning focused, the heartbeat of a local church congregation changes when five-fold (Eph 4:11) gifted leaders train and develop their people to individually see God's amazing grace transform hearts and lives in the loved ones, friends, neighbors, and local community networks within their reach. A church finds encouraging change when its members begin sharing their own faith at work or over meals and beholding people accept Christ as their personal Savior. Train your members to understand how and when to share with others their personal journeys with God. Our society has become so worried about offending someone that the culture shift has somehow suggested to God's people that sharing their faith is inappropriate. Nonsense! People who have been changed by a genuine relationship with the Lord, who understand that their sins have been forgiven and thrown into the sea of never remembering again, are the ones committed to telling others the Good News! When your own people begin to pray with friends, see life-transformation, and witness burdens lifted, your church will be well on its way to renewal and to having fresh portraits of encounter! That, friends, sets the atmosphere for the day of worship for any attendee whose heart is focused on the Lord; as well it sets the atmosphere for any guest—possibly a first-time attender—or even a "this was their first time and the only time they were planning on coming" attender—to experience the wonderful presence of God in a palpable and most personal way.

The last several paragraphs have given some insight to the first four bullets listed at the beginning of this chapter:

1. Praise and Worship,
2. Anointed Preaching of the Word,
3. Missions, and
4. Soul-winning.

I'll briefly address these next four:

5. Prayer,
6. Discipleship,
7. Serving, and
8. Reproducing/Planting.

These four are the foundation that the initial four are built upon.

Prayer

Prayer is foundational to anything in ministry. Prayer is key for anything spiritually noteworthy or heaven-influenced. One's worship service is little more than talent, and atonal at best, without adequate time in prayer. Preaching without first praying is futile and unbiblical. Jesus Christ said, "Apart from me, you can do nothing" (John 15:5). Preaching without spending time with the Lord in prayer is powerless and Spirit-presence-empty. It was common for the Apostle Paul to ask the churches he worked among for prayer that his

> *Preaching without first praying is futile and unbiblical.*

ministry in the Word would be courageous and effectual. See Ephesians 6:19 and Colossians 4:3-4. Further, the apostles were themselves totally devoted to "prayer and to the preaching ministry" (Acts 6:4).

Prayer brings the peace of God's presence to calm the soul from strife and daily struggles. Prayer broadens one's faith. It is through prayer that humankind understands God's will and perceives the steps of life's journey. God's omniscience and omnipotence fills the heart of seeking souls as they commune with the One True God, and through prayer, hearts are prepared for His service as He calls them to every good work.

Discipleship

The church is neither being built nor God's Kingdom growing by attaining more churchgoers but by making disciples. A disciple is a dedicated follower of Jesus. Discipleship must be a key process of any church mission whereby the Holy Spirit equips individuals as they grow in the Lord Jesus Christ. The course of discipleship necessitates believers to reply to the Holy Spirit's urging to inspect their opinions, words, and activities and parallel them with the Word of God. This requires that we be in the Word daily, learning, praying, and conforming to that which God's Word offers.

Serving

"For even the Son of Man did not come to be served, but to serve, and to give his life as a ransom for many" (Mark 10:45, NIV). Serving others in the heart and name of Christ does as much for the server as for those being served. Gifts are realized and further developed, joy and peace are experienced, faith is increased, and God's presence is recognized as we give of ourselves to others. Some think they have little to offer. Scripturally, little becomes much. "But thou, Bethlehem Ephratah, though thou be little among the thousands of Judah, yet out of thee shall he come forth unto me that is to be ruler in Israel; whose going forth have been from of old from everlasting" (Micah 5:2, KJV). Use what you have and watch God do miracles through it. Dorcus had a needle, Mary had a small alabaster box of ointment, the poor widow owned two mites, young David the shepherd held a sling and five small stones. What do you possess that you can give for others?

Reproducing/Planting

Five-fold ministry (Eph 4:11) includes apostolic callings. Over the years much research has been done to help determine that planting new churches is the most strategic way of reaching more individuals for Christ. New churches grow faster than do older congregations. I'm even a strong proponent that more types of churches are needed to reach a growing and culturally diverse demographic. Quite simply said, church planting is the major activity in the New Testament and remains to date as the most effective evangelistic method on earth. As a denominational

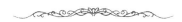

Church planting is the major activity in the New Testament and remains the most effective evangelistic method on earth.

superintendent, I have personally witnessed that it is easier to give birth to a new congregation, full of life and vitality, than it is to revitalize a church on the downhill turn of its lifecycle. I believe in church multiplication. Churches who plant churches, who plant churches, trust God to do the miraculous. Have faith. Watch in astonishment as God does what people cannot not fathom. Plant churches.

Chapter 16

Navigating a Name Change

Have you considered changing the name of your church? Are there such encouraging things occurring in the church that a new name would quite simply better communicate who you are to the community? Does the past simply have such a negative connotation that you and your leadership believes there's no other way to overcome the stigma of community perception (to whatever occurred previously) in your church's history? That's very sad—mostly for the community, those who are not followers of Christ, and any who may have been duped by unscrupulous leaders who failed in leading people with integrity to Jesus. It's sad because many people give up on God when they see people they trust who have failed them in one way or another. We should all remember to never give up on God just because a person you trusted may have missed the mark. Our eyes are best focused when they stay on Jesus. If your church has experienced those types of difficulties, however, then you may be correct in considering that a name change or a whole new start might be the way to go. It is possible that a fresh start could be your ticket to regaining strength and trust. Let me offer one quick side note, though, before you go down that aisle.

As much as building a new building doesn't grow a church, keep in mind that a name change doesn't change or alter the reality of the actual ministries (good or bad) that your church is offering. Sometimes a name change will work for what you're hoping to accomplish, but sometimes it does not. I'd suffice to say that usually, it does not. What matters most is what's happening inside the church—and outside the church—rather than the name on the door. If you need to change your church's stigma in the community, then change the ministry, strengthen it, build trust again, do something meaningful for the community and the demographic environs around your city. Make a difference for the Kingdom. If you do that, people will notice, perceptions will change, and the name on the door will become secondary to the power in the house.

I was attending a church leadership conference in Mexico in early 2019. The speaker drew attention to statistical analysis on churches since 2009 that had opted for removing denominational-specific titles for what they perceived as more culturally relevant names. For instance, a community church known for decades as, "XYZ Baptist, XYZ Methodist, XYZ Assembly of God, and so forth," changing their names for titles such as, "XYZ Church, Community Fellowship," etc. Now, if your church happens to be named such as one of the examples, smile and know that I am not picking on you at all. Rather, I am simply making a point that at this conference, the speaker noted statistics indicating that, as these churches changed their names, or took the brand logo off their sign, they discovered a significant *decrease* in the number of people listed in their statistical categories for conversions, water baptisms, Spirit baptisms, etc.

It might do us all well, regardless of our brand loyalty, to consider just that: Brand Loyalty. It appears there is reason to believe that culture around us is leaning again toward wanting to know exactly what kind of church that might be as they drive by the church sign. I believe people want to know (to the best of their perception, at least) who we are and what we believe. From a quick passing glance of a sign or logo they should not have a sense that we're trying to hide something from them or keep them wondering about the details of who we might be. I'm a proponent of putting the affiliation's name of the local church *back* on the sign, if in fact a church is actually affiliated with a particular denomination or ecclesial covering—and apparently there are statistics to indicate the benefit of doing so.

I believe people want to know who we are and what we believe.

I remember years ago when pastoring, our church had changed its name. Known for many years by a certain name with a brand-specific logo and title, we kept our spiritual covering, remained true to our doctrinal purity, and changed little as to our approach to ministry in the area. We simply removed the denominational title and logo from the signs and materials, opting for a more community-based marketing approach. A few years later, a church guest gave a sizable offering one Sunday morning. As pre-arranged with our bookkeeper, if a sizable monetary gift was given that our computer system didn't recognize as from a regular donor or which was flagged as a unique and large gift, I was to be informed so I could quickly respond to the donor with an expression of personal appreciation and conversation.

I called the church guest and received a wonderful conversation regarding how they had thoroughly enjoyed our church, the worship, the preaching, and the presence of the Lord. The newcomer to the church continued to say how they were more so encouraged to have heard me from the pulpit acknowledge openly our denominational affiliation and my love for the flag (so to speak). I came to learn that they had been driving for a couple of years from our community to a neighboring city nearby, attending a church they didn't love all that much, simply because our church sign was not detail-specific as to our denominational affiliation. They had had no idea as they drove past our sign every day what group we were affiliated with. They hadn't wanted to subject their family to any unknowns. However, they had been looking for the denomination they had participated in before moving from Texas, and someone had recently told them they thought our church was affiliated with that exact group. I thanked them for their kind comments, their large gift, and their attendance. They assured me they had found their new church home and would return for worship weekly. They were true to that promise. Maybe there is something to having our affiliation listed again on our signs. Yes, I soon changed our signs to include our denominational logo.

Chapter 17

Leading from the Pastor's Home

There's no doubt, as has been mentioned in earlier chapters, that maintaining integrity is the most vital matter for those called to God's purposes. With all the sexual misconduct cases being dealt with by victims across the globe, it's heartbreaking to think of the hurt that's been caused and the damage that's been done to individuals' lives, families' futures, and the Church as a whole by those who claim to be pastors, priests, or leaders of God's Church. How do you know or discern whether leaders, in their own homes, are who they say they are? I've always said you can tell a lot about people by spending five minutes in their home, looking for sixty seconds at their checkbook register, or talking to their two- to six-year-old children. (Children tell everything.)

Through the years Renee has always been quick to say, "Never say anything about someone else's children." By the grace of God, there go we, or ours. When children seem to wander from the hope you instilled or the values you offered, keep in mind, love them always, pray fervently, and realize you can't carry the weight of the burdens from decisions they choose to make, often as adults. You can't blame yourself for choices others make. There comes a time when children become adults and make their own decisions, right or wrong, healthy or unhealthy, within your personal value systems—or without. Prodigals need love. Prodigals need prayer.

That said, we do know still that some good people have bad apples in their families. While there are things families can do to prepare a path for their children or lay a foundation of trust for their lives, it is good to remember that none of us can be held accountable for the decisions of another. Second, some bad people have good apples in their families. The Redeemer is no respecter of persons. He loves us all, good and bad. He lived and died for us all, including those who have it together, and those who do not. He is available for all—those who call upon Him and those who have yet to whisper or shout His name in humble and repentant prayer. He wishes that none would perish without a personal relationship with Him, and He gave His life that all might come to accept His amazing grace and find healing, peace, joy, and completeness in Him, both here on earth and for all eternity in heaven.

Prodigals need love.
Prodigals need prayer.

Only in the secret place of a personal relationship with God will men and women of the cloth (those leading God's Church) be found faithful. Numbers 16:22 shows Moses's sentiment before God as he prostrated himself before the

Lord and had the people's best interests at heart. Though hardened from witnessing the slave labor and treatment of his people in Pharaoh's kingdom, his journey from the thrones of Egypt to the backside of the desert shepherding sheep turned the hardness of his heart to that which was Spirit empowered. Hebrews 3:2 explained that Moses was faithful in God's house. It would be good for today's church leaders to strive for this faithfulness both in the church and without.

Obviously, the pastor's first priority is making sure one's personal relationship with the Lord is healthy and faithful, but for those who are married, the pastor's family is the most treasurable church he or she will ever lead, so they should always be given the highest priority. The grueling schedules of pastoral leadership, church growth development, discipleship, resourcing, and constant meetings, will drain pastors and steal precious family time. That time with family has to be guarded, scheduled at times, and protected from the constant barrage of committee meetings, phone calls, text messages, and emails. Go to the dance recitals and to the football, baseball, basketball, lacrosse, and soccer games. You get the picture. Someone else can run a meeting once in a while, if necessary. Get away, and build family memories any time possible. When the children are adults they will not remember the toys or the expensive Christmas and birthday gifts with more than a fleeting review of a

> *Get away, and build family memories any time possible.*

photograph. What they will remember is you, the time you spent with them, the memories you built with them, and the love, trust, and hope you shared and instilled in them.

Parents who don't attend church should not be surprised when they raise children who don't know the Lord and have no interest in meeting Him. In my journey, I've found that many of those parents don't recognize nor care so much about the things of God in their earlier years themselves. Only later do they begin recognizing their need for God and often passionately or even desperately wishing their kids would turn their lives around and know the Lord. Maybe that's some of the issue in and of itself. We as individuals cannot turn our lives around. Only God can save, and only the Redeemer can turn our lives around. Later in life, though, our kids begin to reconsider their ways and often open their hearts to God's hope, healing, and salvation. Unfortunately, for their children, they've set the path for their kids to walk, and their kids are walking the path they provided.

I find it peculiar speaking with parents who later in life share concerns that their children are un-churched and uninterested. Yet, the parents themselves never made church attendance a priority in their lives, permitted the things of God and His church to be optional or negotiable, and had minute interest in going to church as a family when the kids were growing up. Then, as adults, their children have little interest for the things of God and consider church attendance meaningless.

If you're living this heartbreak, never give up on your kids. Forgive yourselves for missing the mark in this area, and believe that God can do anything, at any time, as you begin where you are—faithfully trusting and serving Him. Pray for miracles to move mountains, soften hardened hearts, and heal broken and wounded lives. Why do I believe in miracles? I believe in miracles because I believe in God.

Remember, no one is perfect, and no family has it all together. As mentioned earlier, Rence and I have made it a priority in our marriage to try to never judge another couple's children; simply love them and pray for them. We might have opinions, we may have thoughts about one thing or another, but we've worked through the years to specifically avoid judging. On a personal note, I've been accused of judging a few times. Maybe you have been also. But, in my opinion, the plumb line of determining whether you're judging or quite simply stating a fact comes in the simple point of the standards you hold. I've often found that non-believers, or those who would personally consider themselves believers but in my opinion are disregarding certain direct aspects of scripture, will wince and squirm, smile or disregard, any direct statements of loyalty to God, His work, or the Church. So keep in mind that if you hold to biblical faithfulness, godly honor, and righteousness, and if you stand up for Christ and His Church, don't be surprised when you're chastised for judging any other individual who chooses not to live by those standards. If your heart is right and your respect is intact, in reality, you're not judging them. Their lives have judged themselves already, according the Word.

It's helpful not to be offensive if you have a standard that's different from others. I remember years ago I was officially interviewing a candidate who was requesting ministerial credentials. As the denominational superintendent, a colleague and I were meeting with him in the process of his asking for approvals to become a minister in our national fellowship. Years later, I now laugh about it. At the time, I was not laughing.

Within minutes of our sitting down in my office for the credential interview, the candidate began to share that he'd been disturbed to see on my social media post of recent that I had watched the movie *Forrest Gump* with my daughter. He went on further to explain in no uncertain terms that he felt it was sinful and that as a denominational superintendent he was praying for me, that I would ... Well, you get the point. In his opinion, I was sinful and had disappointed him. In my opinion he was ludicrous.

I do give him credit for one thing, though; he apparently had standards. We all need standards. I can respect that he apparently felt a minister should avoid anything on television that would have something worldly in it. For me, I've always been of the opinion that ministers should be in the world, but not of the world. I took a vow to abstain from drinking alcohol, but if I choose to eat, I will be

We all need standards.

purchasing food in a store that sells it because any local grocery store sells alcohol. Maybe in his opinion, I should have grown my own garden and avoided places that offered such worldly vices. My advice is simply that you avoid being offensive with your standards or your questioning of others' standards when disappointed by your superintendent (especially if you're meeting with him or her to ask for approval to receive ministerial credentials).

Chapter 18

Being Boss vs. Being a Leader

In the early days of a new staff member, Melissa, joining our office team, I had to remind her almost daily that I was not her boss. I was her colleague. We were all team members, just with different roles or skill sets. I made it clear that she and the others on our team are far more gifted than I am in the roles they serve. We laugh about the boss thing now, but communicating these things from the start of a person's tenure is certainly a great way to build a strong team. Those who view themselves as "the boss" or "the executive director" or "the one in charge" (and, we've all met them) most usually rub me the wrong way, and it's a challenge to want to work on their team.

I have rarely had a difficult time having an opinion. In my office we sometimes muse that I am too transparent with comments and welcome my team to temper those thoughts whenever they know I need it. We've smiled often, with the tilt of a head indicating that the sentiment was actually serious, when guiding comments were offered. In those moments, staff become teams, employees become confidants, subordinates become colleagues, and the grind becomes teamwork.

Through the years, I have been blessed (for the most part) with loyal, stable, capable, visionary, creative, methodical, and long-term leaders as team players and staff members for the ministries the Lord has granted to my care. When people around you are better than you are, it makes the journey of ministry leadership much more enjoyable, and at times entertaining! Annually, over the past fifteen-plus years, I've offered merit awards for years of service. Each year one of the most encouraging things for me to do is give an award to a team player who has been by my side and/or on the team for five years, ten years, fifteen years, twenty years, twenty-five years, thirty years, and more. It's not uncommon for team members to have been with me for ten to thirty years. I suppose when you do ministry and life with a group of leaders for that many years, you learn to trust one another, glean from one another, and challenge one another to be the best we can be for the Lord's work.

I remember years ago one particular day arriving to work, our church ministry campus (at the time) of nearly forty acres on a main highway with traffic buzzing by at sixty to seventy miles per hour seemed especially messy with trash and debris, as is often the case of major highways in our cities. That particular day, I mentioned to the staff that I was going to head outside to do a few things, and that I'd appreciate them rearranging an hour or so of their morning to come help me. They had no idea what I had in mind, and I didn't exactly tell them what was in store for the team. They quickly determined the game plan as I began walking the roadway, through our acreage, picking up trash. I led the way. They followed. We did it together. We didn't leave it, as if we were too busy to deal with it. We didn't expect someone else to do it. We set a standard ourselves to be and provide our ministries with as much excellence as we could possibly offer. I didn't want to be a boss that day. I wanted to be a leader.

Leaders teach others. Bosses drive them. Leaders function from generosity, care, and liberality. Bosses function from position or from their own expected or exacted authority roles. I have found it laughable through the years that the perceptions of those who perceive themselves in certain ways (I'll call them "bosses" here) are viewed quite differently from most of the people working for them. Notice, I didn't say, "working with them." There's little togetherness in those types of structures. There are few teams in those systems. Typically such a work environment is doors closed, all business, few laughs, and rare offers of opinions—since the thought is, "There's no need to offer it, if I'm just going to be shut down anyway."

> *Leaders function from generosity, care, and liberality. Bosses function from position.*

Leaders encourage and produce eagerness, interest, and anticipation, while bosses generate frustration, anxiety, and trepidation. Leaders are proactive, thinking ahead to what the team will need tomorrow, or next week. Bosses expect things done, expect things perfect, and expect things as they want them. They are frustrated when even they have dropped the ball, assuming that one of their staff should have worked harder or smarter to make sure something was accomplished. Those are the people I don't want to work for!

Leaders say, "We're going to..." while bosses say, "I'm expecting you to..." Sometimes bosses focus on "I" rather than "we." When things don't go as hoped, planned, or expected, bosses usually find fault, and quickly reprove or correct for work done improperly. Leaders are resolute, discovering the setbacks and elevating the whole. Leaders find a way of bringing peace and a challenge to excellence in the situation, even if it's "all hands on deck" time. Leaders show. Bosses know. Leaders cultivate and improve people. Bosses simply use people for their own advancement or purposes without acknowledging the genuine gifts and efforts offered. Leaders offer recognition and praise. Bosses take credit. Leaders ask. Bosses demand. Some of the greatest leaders I've met still remember to say, "Please," and "Thank you." Bosses occasionally don't even look you in the eye, are cutting with their comments, or forget the dignity of human care and concern.

Are you a boss or a leader? I am reminded of the apostles and their leadership so exemplified in Acts 2. It is amazing how the Lord used them in unity, and how the people followed their example as God's favor and blessings fell on them all!

> 42 They devoted themselves to the apostles' teaching and to the fellowship, to the breaking of bread and to prayer. 43 Everyone was filled with awe, and many

wonders and miraculous signs were done by the apostles. 44 All the believers were together and had everything in common. 45 Selling their possessions and goods, they gave to anyone as he had need. 46 Every day they continued to meet together in the temple courts. They broke bread in their homes and ate together with glad and sincere hearts, 47 praising God and enjoying the favor of all the people. And the Lord added to their number daily those who were being saved (Acts 2:42-47, NIV).

While I certainly cannot speak for the dozens who have worked with me through the years, I would like to hope I've offered more of the positives in this chapter than the negatives. While no one is perfect or scoring a hundred every week, each of us can strive to be better year-to-year.

To the many staff and team members who've led with me, done ministry with me, dreamed dreams with me, and developed ministries, with me through the years, I hope you can look back and say, "He considered me a valued team member, an equal, a colleague, at times a gift in the journey, and a trusted voice in the wilderness as we worked together for Kingdom purposes." As I said, none of us hit a homerun all the time when it comes to these efforts, but it's worth the challenge to remind oneself that leaders are much more readily followed than are bosses. Be a leader, not a boss.

Be intentional about your leadership. Do things on purpose. Be deliberate. Treat people the right way, and for the right reasons.

Chapter 19

Protecting Children and Following Ministerial Ethics

I t was 2004, and I had been elected a state superintendent for the denomination I serve. At the church I had
served for sixteen years previously, when new facilities
had been built, I had the architects design large glass
windows in all of the offices.

On the first day entering my new superintendent's
office, I smiled, knowing I'd be making a change almost
immediately. The office door, as with the other office doors
in the facility, were all solid doors. There were no glass
inserts to allow anyone to look inside. To me, that was a
problem. It is imperative to serve, counsel, minister, and
pray with integrity, at times with complete confidentiality,
and on occasions with strategic purpose, so that anyone
walking by outside the doors with a simple glance can determine who's in the room and exactly what's occurring. There
should never be a moment when anyone could find oneself
alone, or where anyone else would be placed in a position of
potentially questioning your being in an office alone with

another person, certainly with minors, or whatever the case would be that could involve a question of integrity.

As soon as I could work out the details to get it accomplished, I had all the office doors—including mine—removed, altered, and glass windowpanes inserted. I was eliminating the opportunity for the enemy to catch me or anyone else in our office off-guard in a compromising or even questionable situation. Though my office door is typically open, and I've always led with an "open door policy," this renovation would make sure I was never closed off or alone in my office without others being able to see easily into the office at will.

The purpose of this brief chapter is to simply cause church leaders to re-think their structures, procedures, and standard operating practices. It is important for ministers to dedicate themselves to conduct, principles, and codes of ethics in Christian service that allow their lives to be a trusted voice and witness to those around them. Ensuring integrity carries with it various responsibilities to numerous groups and begins with oneself. Only you can commit to your own devotional life, emotional health, physical regimen, time management, continuing education or growth tracks, financial honesty, or Christ-like attitudes to give you influence and voice within and without the church and the local community.

Ensuring integrity carries with it various responsibilities

Through decades of ministry, I've been reminded that I carry responsibilities not only for my actions and integrity, but to protect the heart and trust of those who matter the most in my own life—my wife and children, the church I pastored, the denomination I lead, the hundreds of colleagues I serve, and the thousands of congregants in churches that look to my office and role for trust and guidance, faithfulness and integrity. That's a lot to take in when thinking about the serious nature of misconduct. I suppose what has always kept me most focused is the devotion and love I have for my wife and children. As a superintendent, I've seen families destroyed, children fall away from their parents and the church, and good people throw up their hands in disgust, walking away from all they'd known as truth and family, because of the mistakes, sin, and horrific pain caused by ministers lacking in the ethics department. It's time for the Church and her leaders to make integrity a priority again.

I've heard heart-wrenching stories of parishioners taken advantage of by clergy. I'm well aware of the pain caused when youth or children's pastors would be driving a group of children or teens (minors) home from church-related outings and somehow the last teen to be dropped off at her home would be a teenage girl

It's time for the Church and her leaders to make integrity a priority again.

(driven home alone – at that point – by (in this case) their single, or married, male youth pastor). Of course, the story could be a female staff member and a male teen or child, as well. This scenario is likewise problematic in both opposite-sex or same-sex situations. Is it possible something inappropriate occurred from a youth leader? Is it possible a teen or child could—or would—say that something occurred for some reason, even if it did not? Unfortunately, who will know the truth when there's no witness or accountability? Such scenarios should never occur. Whether anything inappropriate were to have occurred or not, the case for integrity and accountability should always win and be the paramount lesson trusted by every parent and teen/child in a church's care. I have always stood for the care and protection of children and teens; the church and her leaders must commit everything in their power to that end—their protection. Possibly a better overall methodology would be to have parents meet their kids at the church. Either way, there must be a reasonable resolve for integrity at all times.

Chapter 20

Arminianism vs. Calvinism

My early years were formed in the pews of Baptist churches. I can remember as if it were yesterday, my being likely not much more than toddler age, playing with a toy red truck under the pews of the Lily Baptist Church just south of London, Kentucky. My mother played the piano. She was usually up front or on the front row. My father was a deacon and sat habitually about six rows back on the left from the entrance door facing the pulpit, on the extreme left hand side on the end of one of those old wooden pews. There were no seat cushions in those days! I would crawl from time to time to the rows ahead of us, no doubt fumbling around the shoes or the feet of long-term family friends. Other times I would find myself in the rows behind us, as the wheels on that red truck led the way.

Whatever happened to the days of our children growing up under the pews? What happened to the days where our children grew up with memories of their dads kneeling in prayer? I remember my dad getting down on his knees when he'd pray in that pew each week. The pastor then, during the mid 1960s, was Hargus Shackelford; he was a trusted family friend to my father. He would begin to pray, and the church would follow in. My dad would immediately kneel, as if it were expected as something everyone was supposed to do. I would quietly bring my truck to a halt, knowing I'd be in some equivalent of trouble if I were to cause too much noise or bring a stir of attention at that holy moment.

Little did I recognize in those years the foundation being laid by the doctrine and teaching I was overhearing week to week. Calvinism was not something I knew anything about at the time. The Calvinist concept of TULIP was unheard of; the only tulip I knew about was the flower my parents would speak about from time to time. The Wesley family was something that only many years

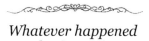

Whatever happened to the days of our children growing up under the pews?

later I would learn about, as they became somewhat related to or connected to the ideologies of deprivation, conditional election, unlimited atonement, resistible grace, or assurance and security.

Knowing that a myriad of ecclesiastical backgrounds and opinions fill the landscape of my present family and friends, my point in this chapter is not so much to question whether one should surrender to Calvinism or lean the other direction and adhere to my own preferred Classic Pentecostalism, or even one's trusted Wesley-Arminian convictions. I'll get to that in a moment. The books I write are for everyone regardless of denominational or theological convictions. While I certainly have my own preferences and determined biblical interpretations, I find it imperative for each of us to find our own way to the Cross. It seems to me far too many church leaders are illiterate to the fundamental and foundational elements of their own faith. To that end, I write this chapter to offer some elementary element of clarification regarding theological and doctrinal positions often misunderstood. Seek Him, and He will answer you.

So, what exactly did John Wesley or John Calvin proclaim, you might say? The "T" of Calvinism's TULIP stands for Calvin's *Total Depravity*, which declared mortal beings as so affected by the destructive penalties of original sin that they are powerless of being blameless and are continuously and unchangeably sinful. Freedom for humankind is considered wholly enslaved by sin so we can simply choose malevolence. Wesley's concept of *Deprivation* offered something less than *Total*. In the substance established by the Dutch Reformed theologian, Jacobus Arminius, human beings are immoral and certainly sinful without God, powerless on their own of being morally virtuous or righteous. Nevertheless, they are not hopelessly or insuppressibly sinful and can be changed and renewed by God's grace. In Wesley's premise, God's prevenient grace regenerates to humanity the freedom or liberty of will.

Far too many church leaders are illiterate to the foundational elements of their own faith.

The "U" of Calvinism's TULIP addresses the point of Unconditional Election. With the premise that humankind cannot select for themselves, God by His immortal judgment has selected or designated some to be deemed as blameless or righteous, minus any conditions assigned to that election. As I understand it, Wesley argued that God had chosen all humanity to be holy and righteous solely by His grace, yet that He has called us to respond to that grace by applying our God-restored human choice as a condition of adored election. Wesley did not preach predestination, nor believe that certain individuals had been pre-elected by God for salvation and somehow others for damnation. He fully avowed that salvation was simply conceivable by the sovereign grace of God.

Augustine, of Hippo (modern Algeria), the fourth-century church father (354 – 430 AD), established the foundational principles of John Calvin's work. The "L" of Calvin's TULIP refers to the offer of a *Limited Atonement*. We are all grateful that God forgave sinful humanity and that from Christ's death on the Cross, burial, and resurrection, God offers forgiveness for all of humanity. Therein, however, came the theological debate of the centuries, as to *who* within humanity was *included* in that forgiveness. Calvin's work proclaimed that the Atonement was limited only to those God had chosen. Wesley argued vehemently against such a proclamation, preaching that the effects of the Atonement are freely available to all those God has chosen. Wesley went on to define those as including *all* humanity, "whosoever will."

Irresistible Grace, the "I" of Calvin's TULIP, teaches that the grace God extends to all humankind to affect their select position, or their election, is not something that can be refused, since it has been declared or ordered by God. Wesley denounced this teaching, defining the Scriptures as imparting solely God's grace as free and offered without merit. However, Wesleyan theology taught that people are granted freedom by God to accept or refuse His amazing grace. Therein is the foundation of salvation—unmerited favor accepted or rejected.

Finally, the Calvin TULIP presents *Perseverance of the Saints* as the statement that God's elect, decreed by Him and irresistible from His grace, are unconditionally and eternally secure in that election. This is where the church world receives the concept, "Once saved, always saved." While it should not be considered so simplistically, this has often become the standardized tenet for defining Calvinism. Wesley, of course, interpreted Scripture to say that there is assurance and security for the believer in God's grace for salvation, but that that security is relative to sustained and continuous fidelity and faithfulness to God's Word and His biblical decrees. Just as one can choose to accept God, one can always and defiantly choose to reject God.

If you'd never previously thought about the exact distinctions between the two renowned theologies, hopefully this brief explanation offers insight for your further study. But, here's the kicker for this book's purposes and this chapter. I've used Calvin and

My point is to say, doctrine matters.

Wesley to discuss some key themes I truly believe every

person should take to heart. It's not so much that I'm encouraging one to espouse one position over another (though I clearly fall into the Wesley-Arminian family); rather I simply want to address my basic foundation and hope for all. Far too many people attend churches and have no idea what their church theology addresses. My point is to say, doctrine matters. The Scripture offers us this commission:

> 9 "Whosoever transgresseth, and abideth not in the doctrine of Christ, hath not God. He that abideth in the doctrine of Christ, he hath both the Father and the Son. 10 If there come any unto you, and bring not this doctrine, receive him not into your house, neither bid him God speed" (2 John 1:9-10, KJV).

Since I've been in ministry there has been a marked shift in the way mainline culture, especially North American, adheres to long-term family loyalties for brand and label. It appears rare to find those who choose to remain strict adherents to a specific foundation and doctrinal purity. Whether one chooses the traditional family church or not, though, the key is, doctrine matters. Truth matters.

I want to encourage today's church attenders to think again about what they believe, why they believe it, and more importantly, to define with confidence what the Bible says about one topic or another. Many attending their church of choice today disregard foundational doctrines of a church to accommodate and assimilate for purposes of a given children's ministry, worship styles of the music and services, and/or the professionalism or graciousness and acceptance found from ministry staff and leaders. It's time to focus again on that which will guide the family far into the future—and into eternity. When times are challenging and questions linger in the valleys of life the balance is found in God's Word. Doctrine matters. Find out what the church you're choosing to attend believes and determine if you agree that it adheres with scriptural truth. How will you know? Read the Bible. Ask questions. Inquire of trusted, church-attending, Bible-reading, genuine Christ-following mentors as to what you should be asking and what they encourage you to be asking. The Bible teaches there is wisdom in counselors, so use those in your life to help you set a high standard that will bring strength to your home and family. Meet with your pastor and ministers at the church to inquire about questions that matter. Finally, trust that if you ask the Father, He will answer. Doctrine matters.

Chapter 21

Providing Premarital and Marital Counseling

Through the years I made it a personal policy to not perform wedding ceremonies where the couple had not given some reasonable effort and dedication to premarital counseling. The commitment I saw in young couples time and again, willing to drive after long days of work multiple hours to arrive for an evening counseling session, gave me the sense that they would in their own marriage journey stand the trials of time.

Of course, there were others who scoffed at the thought of my asking for counseling sessions. Too many of those today have not lasted in their marital bliss. For those people who are years into their marriage struggling with various issues of life together, find a pastor. Find a counselor. Find your hope again. Bring

Find one another's love language.

back the little things you did for one another when you dated. Find one another's love language, and serve one another in the love of Christ.

After decades of ministry, I still believe couples should prepare better for one of the greatest journeys of their lives. Thus, I offer here a few simple suggestions for every couple considering marriage:

- Mark out the word "divorce" from your dictionary.
- Set the moment for the important discussions.
- Find a church and attend together faithfully.
- Tithe and trust God principles.
- Build a savings account.
- Love and forgive.
- Have mentors who are trustworthy and will speak the truth in love.
- Believe in your spouse, and show him or her that you do.
- Make your relationship more important than your careers.
- The biggest gift you can give your children is to love their mother or father, so do it!
- If you've had a failure in an area before, get it right the next time. God redeems if you'll let Him.
- Live within your means.
- Make decisions together, not separately.
- Have your own escapes, but find things you love to do together.
- Develop prayer.
- Add music to your marriage's daily routine. It is therapeutic and simply adds beauty.

Chapter 22

Managing Conflict

Whe you commit your life to leadership, whether through management roles in the modern work force, or in clerical/pastoral duties to God's Church across the globe, you will quickly identify conflict as part of the equation. When I entered the ministry I had no suspicion I'd ever need an attorney. Before my pastoral years concluded, however, I had found more than one occasion when I needed legal counsel. Some may have thought I also needed counseling as I walked through some of those matters, but certainly having a few affable esquires at my disposal became key at various moments. If you face such moments yourselves, remember certain basic scriptural principles. The eternal God is interested in your troubles, and the steps of the righteous are ordered of the Lord.

A good place to begin is with apologies. If you find yourself in the wrong, to any extent, apologize, and do so genuinely. That goes a long way to admitting your humanity and strengthening character and trust. It's customary to identify your personal share of the conflict—and don't delay things. Deal with whomever and whatever immediately and personally. Delaying things or brushing it under a rug, so to speak, doesn't make it go away. It only lingers, the smells get worse, the anger gets more hostile, and the mold grows.

Anytime someone manufactures change, conflict can arise and often does. Change is a natural and indispensable piece of preparing your church for her future. Unfortunately, when conflict arises, rather than learning the art of managing it, too many of today's leaders prefer to ignore stark realities or they hide from conflict, isolating themselves and others from addressing core issues.

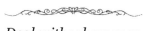

Deal with whomever and whatever immediately and personally.

I heard a professor once remind a class, "Without conflict there would be no New Testament." What a profound truth. Amid the beauty and peace we like to proclaim from Scripture, the road to finding it is paved with war, battles, destruction, and death. Christ dying on the Cross is often captured in messages of a "Good Friday" motif. That's a peculiar name for a day depicting the death of Christ. Thus, conflict is a normal part of the journey to our finding life more abundantly with joy, hope, and peace. There is always a breaking before there can be a healing. Conflict has a way of making us stronger and more resilient. Conflict oddly and optimistically matures us for more effective and efficient work for Christ.

We live in a postmodern culture that invites questions

and questioning. While a number of leaders are receptive, many others unfortunately try to eliminate the questions or feel challenged by them, which is worse. It has not been an easy lesson to learn, but through the years I've become slightly better at recognizing that someone questioning the how and why of my way or our team's process is not really the same as their being threatening or directly argumentative. People simply want to know why, how, when, or can it be done differently and more efficiently for our desired or even better outcomes? The best leaders, in my opinion, give people the respect of answers, dialogue, and open door policy for channeling tools, training, and resourceful resolve. I have on occasion encountered leaders who are out of their element, wrought with varying personal, budgetary, or personality issues, and who simply find themselves afraid to ask for help all because of the potential of that help exposing their weaknesses to the world. That kind of behavior results in an unfruitful leadership style that stifles growth, ingenuity, and the visionary progress. When conflict is well-managed, new routes for ministry can be positive, progressive, and affirming. Perhaps more importantly, problems can be resolved and steps undertaken to advance vision and efforts.

When leaders are threatened by conflict, insecure, or inclined to demonstrate frustration or resentment, the divergence makes matters worse almost every time. One cannot run from conflict, hide it, disguise it, delegate it, or ignore it. Leaders lead. Without addressing conflict, you will create dysfunctional teams that are void of harmony, production, or inspiration.

This brief chapter isn't designed to be the complete answer guide to all your conflicts, but it would help us here to offer a brief crash course in conflict management. When it occurs—and it will—how should you begin the task of resolving it? Initially, recognize you have to deal with it. It cannot be brushed aside, masked, or ignored.

Whether dealing with conflict in the secular or ecclesiastical context, leaders must learn to be generous with forgiveness. People hold onto their bitterness and frustrations from hurts that have been done toward them.

Leaders must learn to be generous with forgiveness.

It's not uncommon for individuals to bring up time and again grievous troubles or charges that had been leveled against them in years past. When they do so, it shows to some extent that they give worth to the pain and have simply not let it go. Jesus encouraged forgiveness. So should we. Further, forgiving another protects your own well-being and keeps the enemy from gaining traction. Be forgiving, and help others to do likewise.

When someone comes to you complaining of overhearing something about someone else, or telling you about what a certain person has done wrong, send that person directly back to the one they're talking about to discuss it themselves. If a conflict isn't yours, but belongs to others, then don't enable bad behavior. Direct others to address their own conflict.

What if you're so frustrated and upset you decide to resign? Keep these simple thoughts in mind. Never resign unless you mean it. If you're on the management side receiving a resignation, always accept it if it's offered to you. As well, teach your people to understand both of these principles. It helps to go cool off before becoming reactionary. Then you can instead be relational and redemptive.

Finally, how does the Bible say to handle conflict? A number of passages deal directly with the matter of disagreements. Hebrews 12 speaks of God's discipline of His children. His discipline is not punitive, but restorative. The Apostle Paul wrote of restoring a faulty and likely broken brother in meekness and with gentleness (Gal 6:1). Although it is with gentleness, you still have to do it.

The Old Testament also addresses how to deal with confrontational issues (Lev 19:17). Likely the most definitive biblical passage germane to the topic is found in Matthew 18. Verse 15 says to go directly to the person with whom conflict has arisen. If that doesn't take care of things amicably, verse 16 says to take a neutral witness (accountability is always a good thing for both parties) for another try. If that doesn't work, verse 17 addresses taking matters to church leaders (for conflicts among believers that may occur). Keep in mind, however, that there is no need to involve people in the matters who need not be involved. It was explained to me once that in my dealing with conflict, I should learn to keep the circles of discussion or influence as small as possible. A professor once described it as "the circle of confession." It only needs to be as big as the circle of offense. Zealous leaders occasionally overlook that the purpose of church discipline is renewal. Our role as leaders is to bring healing. May we always live our lives to restore others and build bridges for hope.

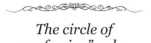

The circle of confession" only needs to be as big as the circle of offense.

I heard it said once, "Just because people have had a difficult life does not give them license to treat people inappropriately." Teach, model, develop, forgive, mediate, and pray toward resolve. Remember, conflict in itself is not sin, but it can certainly set the stage for it.

A number of superb resources and researchers have offered volumes on conflict management and resolution. Avail yourself of those resources and study them. It will be worth the effort in building God's people and His Kingdom.

Chapter 23

Being Submissive, Accountable, and Humble

Three simple words that can change the course of your direction, bring favor to your cause, and provide peace like a river to your heart are the attributes of being submissive, accountable, and humble. I end this book with a brief synopsis of these three unassuming, yet profound adjectives—words I have shared many times with friends, counselees, mentees, and parishioners. These foundations will be steadying pillars for your journey regardless of what challenges you are faced with overcoming.

These foundations will be steadying pillars for your journey

People often ask, "Pray that..." "Pray for me that they will..." "Pray I will..." "How can I know if..." "I wish I could tell if..." Simply remember these three statements before you go into your meeting, before you offer your answers, before you tell them what you really think (so to speak): *Be submissive. Be accountable. Be humble.*

Submissive

To be submissive does not mean you agree to slavery, bondage, or oppression in subjection to another's demands. Rather, it is to be ready to conform to the authority or will of others, to be gently obedient, compliant, malleable, and accommodating or amenable. Each person by nature has his or her opinions, and rightly so, but all of us need to willingly at times submit to others' best interests at times and put our desires behind another's. Though most of us feel we've got it all figured out and that we certainly don't need someone else "who clearly doesn't get it" directing us toward a plan that bogs us down, the reality is that most of us are wrong from time to time. We actually *do* need others speaking into our lives. Submitting to the authority of others who God has placed in our lives is a spiritual principle that many overlook when they feel they've "finally arrived and are prepared themselves to guide their own paths." I believe God provides coverings for us in our lives. It's our duty to God to discern the depths of those coverings; then, through His Word we can better understand our course of action and steps ahead. Spiritually speaking, believers completely give up their will and subject their thoughts and deeds to the will and teachings of Christ.

Accountable

To be accountable speaks of the nature of being responsible and willingly justifying for the actions of decisions. A person with this attribute willingly accepts responsibility for actions. This esteemed characteristic is not something that can be given to you or anyone else. It is a personal trait that distinguishes one from the rest.

Leaders make decisions. Leaders take responsibility for their actions and decisions. Leaders make sure they've processed, prayed, and purposed before making decisions. Have you ever met anyone who seems to blame others or immediately push things off on someone else rather than owning his or her own responsibilities? I certainly have, and it's not a pleasing character trait to witness.

Humble

To be humble is to offer a modest estimate of one's own importance. It is to be respectful, self-effacing, unassertive, deferential, unpresuming. Humility is often considered the opposite of pride. Humility is an outward expression of an appropriate inner regard. Talk less and listen more. Wait a little longer, and go last in line. Ask for counsel and advice. Praise others. Compliment those around you when appropriate. Give credit to others as needed. Own your mistakes, and admit failures. We all have them. Be forgiving, and ask for forgiveness when needed. The Bible speaks of humility. You can do your own thorough search in Scripture on this topic, but don't forget these key passages:

Proverbs 11:12, "With the humble is wisdom," and 1 Peter 5:5, "Clothe yourself with humility toward one-another."

Conclusion

These twenty-three chapters have offered insights into various elements of the practical, systematic, and spiritual sides of church leadership. Parts of it were very personal and a reflection of my own journey. Other segments may have seemed challenging to you. Now, you must use what you've processed to best fit your ministry calling and assignment. Use what you can to strengthen your work for Christ. Critically important is to recognize that everything we do should be covered in prayer. Seek God's presence, and allow the Holy Spirit to guide your church in every situation and service. As I wrote in the first book, God can do more in one blink of the eye than we can do in days, weeks, or months of preparations. Make prayer a priority.

Everything you do should be covered in prayer, allowing the Holy Spirit to guide your church in every situation.

Every person reading this book will find unique elements of it that spark interest or bring opportunity for reflection about what and why we do what we do. Find what you're dedicated to in God's Kingdom, and devote maximum effort to fulfilling

Honor God. Celebrate your people.

those things He's called you to do. Churches are distinctive and divinely intended for select purposes. Honor God. Celebrate your people. Work within your gifts and skillsets to do something amazing for God! Remember—He's cheering you on!

Now, begin your lists, the considerations of specifics that can be done to enhance your ministry experiences and services after you've reviewed our chapter discussions.

Review Questions

For this section, just as I said in Volume 1 of *Setting the Atmosphere for the Day of Worship,* remember that you're not trying to compare yourself with the church down the street or the larger ministry that "has it all." Our desire as church leaders is to honor God with excellence in the things that we can do.

Here are a few questions to help you get started toward making your ministries the best they can be for the Lord. If your church is rural, metropolitan, mobile, traditional, contemporary, High-Church, or a myriad of alternative options for church start-ups or revitalizations today, there are numerous things you can do to shine your brightest and exalt Christ.

Don't skip this important next step. Reading about options offers our heart and minds some considerations that we may have wanted to implement but just haven't gotten to yet. Reading reminds us of things we have likely thought of before but have simply put off because of time, budgetary restraints, or other reasons.

You're not trying to compare yourself with the church down the street. Our desire is to honor God with excellence in the things that we can do.

other reasons. Taking a pen to draft initial thoughts,

however, gives us the opportunity to plan the changes, schedule the changes, make the changes, and cast exciting vision for the church. Doing so will most always build momentum, energy, and hopefully synergy for growth. Thinking of all that should be enhanced in your context actually builds excitement and strategic projection for the greatest days your church has ever seen. Enjoy the journey!

Chapter Discussions

Chapter 1: Holding the Microphone

- Are you looking for ways to build relationships, synergy, friendships, and appreciation of one another's stories? Everyone has a story.
- Do you have a structure in any of your service gatherings that would allow personal testimonials, the opportunity of allowing parishioners to tell their stories, and/or offer personal words of encouragement to the church as a whole?
- Have you ever been concerned about what someone might say over the microphone and then simply opted to avoid the opportunity altogether to avoid the potential problems that could arise?
- Are you willing or wanting to stretch yourself and allow God to use and speak through members of the church?
- Do you want or need the congregation to notice that they are safe in your guiding leadership?

Chapter 2: Polishing Your Shoes

- Is it time to discuss some proper guidelines for your team?

- Should you polish your shoes, literally?
- Could it be that some etiquette training would be beneficial for you, your staff, and leaders, and even for members of your church as a resource to help them all be more effective and efficient in sharing good news with others?
- Is this chapter actually about polishing one's shoes?
- If not, what is this chapter about from your perspective or opinion(s)?

Chapter 3: Leading Board Meetings

- If you do have regularly scheduled board or elder meetings, what are ways they could be enhanced?
- If you do not have regularly scheduled board or elder meetings, then what is the best way for you to get them planned and scheduled now?
- Have you considered inviting staff to your meetings? Why? Or, why not?
- Do you need your church leadership to build community among themselves as they prepare to lead the congregation toward an upcoming vision or accomplishment?

Chapter 4: Serving Eucharist, The Lord's Supper, Communion

- What are the advantages of offering regularly scheduled Communion to your congregants?

- What are the adverse consequences to the church by going months or years without offering or serving the Lord's Supper?
- Do you offer Communion ministry to shut-ins and elderly?
- If your church has been slack in the area of serving Communion, when are you going to schedule it?
- If Communion is a regular part of your services, what are ways you can enhance it or bring new meaning to your serving of the elements?

Chapter 5: Teaching Tithing: Holy unto the Lord and the Accountability of Finances

- If stewardship means we are the stewards of that which God owns and has placed in our care, then should it not stand to reason that leaders should set the example for such stewardship?
- Are wealthy members or leaders causing the pastor or any church leaders to refrain from doing what's biblical and right in order to protect an income source rather than following scriptural principles of integrity and financial stewardship?
- Have you been concerned over how to handle a leader who has chosen to no longer support the church by way of tithes and offerings?

- Would doing a Bible study and some research on what Jesus had to say about stewardship and giving be helpful to you and/or your church leaders?
- Do you preach systematically about giving, tithes, and offerings?
- Are you as the church pastor or leader pleased with the financial matters of your church?
- What ministries of the church presently addressing this topic are working well?
- What ministries do not work well?
- What ministries need to be added or enhanced immediately?
- Do we have two counters for offerings received?
- Does the treasurer make the bank deposits? If so, should there be a accepted accounting procedure protective firewall for individual accountability and corporate integrity in place delegating that responsibility to someone else?

Chapter 6: Standing In His Presence

- Do you expect to experience God's presence in your ministry and services?
- Do you pace your service schedule to allow time to wait in God's presence and linger in worship, allowing the congregants to simply focus on God?

- What are some ways you could restructure your service schedule allowing more opportunity for these growing-closer-to-God moments?
- What are things in your services you could eliminate altogether to allow more time for more important matters?

Chapter 7: Setting Social Media Dos and Don'ts

- Who in your church can be placed in charge of social media?
- Are there photographers and videographers who you could delegate the task of making sure your social media has visual boost?
- Are the words in your social media presentations/venues spelled correctly?
- Does your social media offer complaining or defensive negativity rather than positive influence and encouragement?
- Does your social media make your church or ministries sound needy?
- How can your church develop a better strategy and brand for your ministry?
- How often are you posting?
- Do you engage your people regularly through social media?

Chapter 8: Celebrating the Voice of Your Spouse: Having Renee on the Platform

- When was the last time you purposefully, as the pastor or church leader, had your spouse with you on the platform to address the audience?
- What are ways your spouse could engage and publicly speak to the congregation?
- Are there opportunities that could be developed for you and your leadership spouse(s) to joint-lead with your various ministry options, introducing a team approach to your people?
- When your spouse offers you a word of caution or consideration, do you meaningfully accept it, or do you tend to brush it off?

Chapter 9: Acknowledging the Value of Affiliation

- Why not lead your church board, elders, staff, and leaders in an exercise of your own, determining the most meaningful factors of affiliation(s) for you and your church?
- How can you and your leadership offer your church's service as a part of the bigger team in your network(s)?
- How can you partner together with those to whom you're affiliated to do even more for Christ?

- How can you set the pace for your church to minister in a broader sense to your region, state, networks, and communities?

Chapter 10: Painting the Children's Church Walls

- Was this chapter about painting walls? Maybe? Maybe not? But, do you need your walls painted? If so, paint them.
- Do you have trusted team members?
- What can you do to build team trust?
- What can you do to offer training for your team?
- How can you make your facilities the most they can be for individuals you want to reach?

Chapter 11: Hiring and Firing

- Do you have team members you're proud of? Tell them.
- Are there team members you know you need to release from their present roles, but you're hesitant to do so? If so, who might they be, and why do you need to release them?
- Have you planned a meeting of your board, elders, or trust colleagues to discuss these things? There's more wisdom in two heads working issues out together.

- Consider having an accountability partner with you when you have that pertinent and all-changing meeting with a staff member.
- Do you need signed documentation? Prepare it in advance.

Chapter 12: Making Nominations, Elections, and Appointments

- Would a nominations committee help in your ministry?
- Who among your leaders could serve in such a role?
- Should your church prepare a more formal policies and procedures manuals related to such topics?
- What are other considerations that you (in your scenario) should be discussing related to these matters?

Chapter 13: Speaking in Other Churches

- How can you as the pastor or leader become more engaged and involved in your own community?
- What ways can you offer to serve the broader community?
- What ministerial fellowships have you not been faithful to attend or interested in participating in that you could make an effort to become intentionally and respectfully involved with?

- What other community ministers could you befriend?
- What other ministers in your community could you consider inviting to share in your church? In what ways could you involve them?

Chapter 14: Looking Up, Looking Down, Looking Across

- What churches can you reach out to assist?
- What do you have in your ministry that you could give to a church in need?
- What churches, pastors, or leaders nearby or within reasonable commuting distance could you shadow, develop a mentoring relationship with, learn from, or get some assistance or resourcing from?
- What are ways your church or ministry could partner with others in your network, fellowship, or community to make a difference?

Chapter 15: Understanding Key Elements for Healthy Church

- How is your church doing in these areas?
- What can you do to develop these ministries?
- Who in the church would be key team members for each considered ministry?
  - Praise and worship

- o Anointed preaching of the Word
- o Missions
- o Soul-winning
- o Prayer
- o Discipleship
- o Serving
- o Reproducing/Planting

Chapter 16: Navigating a Name Change

- Why do you or leaders in your church believe a name change would help the church?
- Would changing the name actually change the depth or breadth of ministry occurring?
- What would changing the church's name communicate to the community?
- Would the name change help the church grow?
- Is the name being considered culturally relevant?
- Is the name being considered a healthy option for the community to understand who you are and with whom you're affiliated?
- Would the proposed name change be a lasting name?

Chapter 17: Leading from the Pastor's Home

- How do you schedule and protect your time while showing priority for your family, spouse, and children?

- Do you interrupt meetings to take family phone calls?
- Are you able to draw important lines between being a pastor and a family member or friend as needed?
- How do you bring balance for your children in their pressure to measure up (because they're being scrutinized with expectations), allowing them to be regular kids like everyone else?
- To have a healthy home life, ministers must learn the art of delegation. How are you doing in that arena?
- What do you do to stay spiritually, physically, emotionally, and mentally healthy?

Chapter 18: Being Boss vs. Being a Leader

- What kind of leader am I (pastor/church leaders)?
- What can I do to better my leadership?
- Do people follow me and my leadership? Why? Do they have to? Or, do they want to? Why?
- How can I better invest in the others who make our church or organization effective and efficient?

Chapter 19: Protecting Children and Following Ministerial Ethics

- What can be done to better enhance your facilities for ministerial ethics?

- Can these things be accomplished with in-house workers, or should they be contracted to outside professionals?

- Are there standard operating procedures or policies that need to be enacted for your ministries and staff? If so, what are they?

- Are there areas of your ministries that could be lacking in integrity? If so, how and what steps should you take to begin rectifying those matters immediately?

- How can you better protect your church or ministry's children?

- How can you better ensure the trust of parents and guardians?

Chapter 20: Grasping Arminianism vs. Calvinism

- Do you know what you believe and why you believe it?

- Do you know why you are _____ (doctrinal affiliation)?

- Have you ever studied in detail the doctrines of the Bible?

Chapter 21: Providing Premarital and Marital Counseling

- Are you willing to admit and encourage others to accept that it's okay to have both a pastor and a counselor simultaneously, if needed?
- Do you require or encourage premarital counseling before you perform wedding ceremonies?
- Do you know of Christian licensed therapists, social workers, or counselors that you can refer families to when their circumstances are dire and you sense they need professional assistance?
- If you need to have any conversation of high importance, how can you best set the moment for the discussion: A quiet restaurant free from distractions? A corner or back table where your spouse can face the wall, not the public or me? Flowers?
- Who are your mentors who will speak the truth in love?
- In what ways have you allowed career or jobs to become more important than your marriage or family relationships?

Chapter 22: Managing Conflict

- Set a time to research and choose two to four books on the subject.

- Do a personality inventory assessment and determine your own unique styles of leadership and conflict management.
- What should you work to change about your styles of handling conflict?
- Are you too harsh with people?
- Do you avoid conflict?
- What does your own approach to conflict management cause in other staff dynamics?
- Are there matters you have not yet fully dealt with that you need to put on the front burner of priorities for your church/organization?

Chapter 23: Being Submissive, Accountable, and Humble

- Would others say that you are submissive?
- Would your accountability partners or those you would consider yourself accountable to consider you as submissive, accountable, and/or humble?
- Does your spouse and family members view you as submissive, accountable, and humble?
- What can you do to work on these areas of life and leadership?

About Joseph S. Girdler, DMin
Superintendent, Kentucky Ministry Network
Assemblies of God (USA)

Education
University of Kentucky, 1984
      BA, Psychology
      BA, Communications

Asbury Theological Seminary, 1991
      MA, Missions & Evangelism

Assemblies of God Theological Seminary of Evangel University, 2018
      DMin in Pentecostal Leadership

Married
Pastor Joe married Renee (Dr. Renee Vannucci Girdler) on June 7, 1986. She was his birthday present, as it was also his 24th birthday. Renee is the daughter of Assemblies of God pastors from eastern Kentucky. Both parents were 100% Italian, with grandparents on both sides of her family migrating to the United States from Italy in the early 1900s.

Having served as chief resident in Family Medicine and

graduating from the University of Kentucky Medical School with honors, Renee is a board-certified family medicine physician with Norton Healthcare Systems in Louisville. She is the former clinic director and vice chair of the Department of Family Medicine at the University of Louisville, as well as the former director of Clinical Affairs and vice chair of the Department of Family Medicine at the University of Kentucky. Her specialties include Women's Health Care and Diabetes, while having further interactions, as well, with International Medicine.

With an extensive background in ministry, she was previously honored by the former general superintendent of the Assemblies of God, Rev. Thomas Trask, and former AG World Missions director, John Bueno, by her selection as the first female in Assemblies of God history appointed to the World Missions Board of the Assemblies of God. She was honored by former general superintendent, Dr. George O. Wood, in receiving the General Superintendent's Medal of Honor, the Fellowship's highest honor for lay individuals in the Assemblies of God (received at General Council 2011, Phoenix, Arizona). Renee was a longtime member of the Board of Directors for Central Bible College and Evangel University. Renee's medical and missions travels/ministries have included Ecuador, Peru, Argentina, France, Spain, Mexico, South Africa, and Belgium.

Personal
- Born: Corbin, Kentucky, June 7, 1962

- High School: Laurel County High School, London, Kentucky. President of Beta Club, 2-year inductee to the Kentucky All-State Concert and Symphonic Bands
- College: Graduate of the University of Kentucky, 1980-1984; 4-year Music Scholarship recipient (trumpet), President UK Band, Vice-President Psi Chi, Mortar Board
- Married: Dr. Renee V. Girdler, 1986
- Children: Steven Joseph Girdler, MD, born 1991 (wife, Julia). Steven is a physician at Mt. Sinai Medical Center, New York, NY, Orthopedic Surgery.
- Children: Rachel Renee Girdler, MSW, born 1995. Rachel is a missionary associate, Ecuador.
- Grandchildren: James Hayes Girdler, born 2019, New York, NY
- Presented "Mayor's Key to the City" – Versailles, Kentucky, 2004.
- Approximately 50 International Mission Trips globally
- Commissioned Kentucky Colonel, by Kentucky Governor Martha Layne Collins, 1986.
- Commissioned Kentucky Colonel, by Kentucky Governor Matt Bevin, 2016.

Ministry

- Superintendent: Kentucky Ministry Network of the Assemblies of God, 2004-Present
- General Presbyter: Assemblies of God USA, 2004-Present
- General Council Assemblies of God USA, Commission on Chaplaincy (2019-2020)
- General Council Assemblies of God USA, Commission on Ethnicity (2014-present)
- General Council Assemblies of God USA, Commission on Evangelism (2005-2006)
- District Missions Director: Kentucky Assemblies of God, 1997-2005
- Ordained: Assemblies of God, Kentucky District Council, 1994
- Senior/Lead Pastor: King's Way Assembly of God, Versailles, Kentucky, 1992–2004
- Associate Pastor, Music, Youth: King's Way Assembly of God, Versailles, Kentucky, 1988-1992
- Chi-Alpha College Campus Associates: Morehead State University, Morehead, Kentucky, 1987-1988

Publications

- Girdler, Joseph S. "Royal Rangers Leaders You Are Appreciated." *High Adventure: The Official Magazine of Royal Rangers* (Summer 2006).

- Girdler, Joseph S., ed. *75th Anniversary: Kentucky District Council Assemblies of God – 2009.* (Crestwood, KY: Kentucky Assemblies of God, 2009).

- Girdler, Joseph S. *A Christian's Pilgrimage: Israel.* http://www.blurb.com/b/6869906-a-christian-s-pilgrimage-israel. ISBN 9781364411534. Blurb Publishing, 2016.

- Girdler, Joseph S. "The Superintendent Leader-Shift from Pastoral to Apostolic Function: Awareness and Training in Leadership Development for District Superintendents in the Assemblies of God USA." DMin proj. Assemblies of God Theological Seminary, Springfield, MO, 2018.

- Girdler, Joseph S., and Carolyn Tennant. *Keys to the Apostolic and Prophetic: Embracing the Authentic and Avoiding the Bizarre.* Crestwood, KY: Meadow Stream Publishing, 2019.

- Girdler, Joseph S. *Redemptive Missiology in Pneumatic Context*. Crestwood, KY: Meadow Stream Publishing, 2019.

- Girdler, Joseph S. *Setting the Atmosphere for the Day of Worship*. Crestwood, KY: Meadow Stream Publishing, 2019.

- Girdler, Joseph S. *Estableciendo La Atmósfera Para El Día De Adoración*. Crestwood, KY: Meadow Stream Publishing, 2019.

- Girdler, Joseph S. *Setting the Atmosphere for the Day of Worship – II*. Crestwood, KY: Meadow Stream Publishing, 2020.

Raised Southern Baptist and Missionary Baptist, and then attending a primarily Methodist seminary, "Pastor Joe" began his ministry on a college campus serving Morehead State University in Morehead, KY, with the Assemblies of God. Followed by four years of music ministry and youth ministry, he was propelled to a lead pastorate in 1992. His welcoming relationships with pastors of multiple fellowships and denominations have served him well in developing a broad and ecumenical approach to church networks globally. Early in ministry he was asked to serve in state-wide denominational leadership. Serving initially as the Kentucky Assemblies of God World Missions director for seven years while simultaneously pastoring King's Way

Assembly in the Lexington, KY, area for a total of sixteen years, Pastor Joe was then elected as the Kentucky Assemblies of God district superintendent in 2004.

Initially a revitalization project, his pastorate with the King's Way congregation found the church overcoming paramount obstacles from the onset, but then underwent three building programs and grew to an average attendance of 400+ people. A key element was that the church grew their missional stewardship from about $15,000 to an annual missions giving of over $430,000 in only twelve years. The last year of his pastorate ('03) the church attained more than $1,000 per capita missions giving, over and above the church's regular tithes and offerings. The church was honored, of well over 12,000 Assemblies of God USA congregations at that time, to achieve Top 100 status in Assemblies of God World Missions giving. Their ministry site by that time of almost forty acres and assets of approximately $4 to $5 million at the time of his transition had become one of the strongest Assemblies of God congregations in the Kentucky Ministry Network of the Assemblies of God. New converts were baptized during the church's morning worship service nearly every Sunday. The church's academic childcare ministry (King's Way Academy) was at the time one of the largest in the region, with over 150 children five days per week and a full-time staff of over twenty-five leaders.

Drs. Joseph and Renee Girdler both serve (presently and previously) on numerous boards and committees throughout the Assemblies of God Fellowship. Their unique journey of together integrating ministry and medicine has offered numerous opportunities to encourage next-generational leadership in the callings of God. Of their many global travels, Joe's mission ministries have included Argentina, Peru, Ecuador (20+ times), Mexico, El Salvador, Brazil, Italy, Germany, Austria, Spain, France, Belgium, England, Turkey, Bulgaria, Egypt, and more.

Contact Information:
Email: jgirdler@kyag.org
Office: +1 (502) 241-7111
Website: www.kyag.org
Meadow Stream Publishing
5501 Meadow Stream Way
Crestwood, KY 40014, USA

Also by the Author

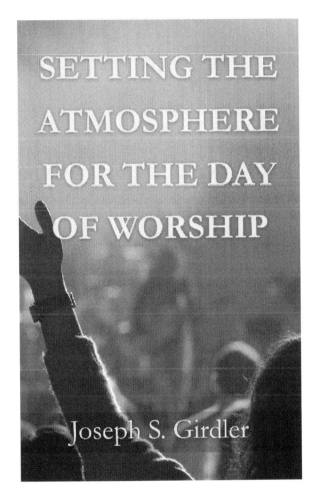

Setting the Atmosphere for the Day of Worship
ISBN: 978-1-7337952-0-3

Estableciendo La Atmosfera Para El Dia De Adoracion
ISBN: 978-1-7337952-6-5

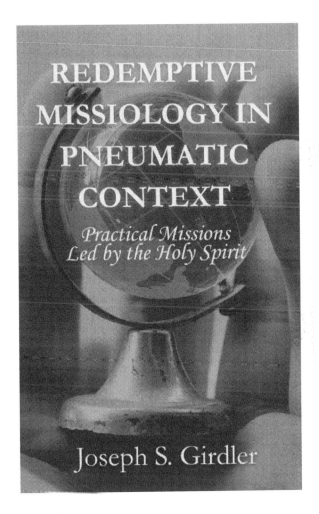

Redemptive Missiology in Pneumatic Context
ISBN: 978-1-7337952-2-7

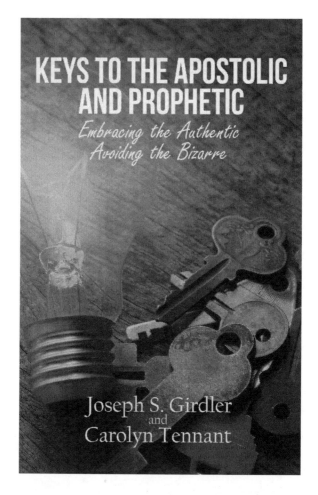

Keys to the Apostolic and Prophetic:
Embracing the Authentic – Avoiding the Bizarre
ISBN: 978-1-7337952-4-1